Derek Naylor

All or N   vt

A

I hope
reading

3ay **Sheffield**
City Council

joy

...ase return/renev
...by the last dat...

*Derek*s may also ...
phone an...

24/5 ...s, ARC 13.

ISBN 978 1901587 97 5

This edition printed and bound in Great Britain by ALD Print Ltd. 297 Sharrow Vale Road, Sheffield, S118ZF

CONTENTS

ACKNOWLEDGEMENTS

I would like to express my gratitude to my editor, proofreader and project manager Laura Anderson for her diligence and patience in piecing together my life story, which I gave her as a hand-written manuscript and in no particular order. Laura has taken my story through to completion of this book, thereby helping me to fulfil my wish to one day see it in print.

I would also like to thank Michael Liversidge for giving his permission to reproduce photographs from his book *Another Wander up the 'Cliffe*. The photographs show my ice-cream van on Banners Corner, and the old herbal medicine shop we turned into The Old Chocolate Shop.

FOREWORD

I met Derek about 25 years ago as a supplier to his business in Sheffield Market. We had an instant rapport, but as in all male friendships, the depth and longevity of the friendship is determined by the female counterparts.

My wife Flo and Derek's wife Joan became very close and so our friendship blossomed, and we spent many a happy evening trying to find (and not always successfully) the best value dinner for two in Sheffield and South Yorkshire.

It was during one of these dinners, or over a bottle of wine or a whisky at my home, that Derek would regale us with tales of his childhood, his extended family and, of course, the various old Sheffield characters that crossed their paths, and I can promise you these people were real characters.

I was so engrossed by these stories that I urged Derek to write them down. In August 2011, while he was recovering from an operation, he brought the first draft of the book to me to read and comment upon. I read it avidly, from first to last page. I was often crying, mostly with laughter but occasionally with sadness and empathy for his childhood life and the sheer brutality of working-class life in Sheffield in the '30s and '40s.

Chaos was ever present in Derek's life, but he was indefatigable and always persevered to overcome any adversity and pick himself up.

You will laugh as you read this book, and you will cry when you read this book, but it is a great tribute to Derek that despite all the tragedy in his life (and I can assure the reader that there is more than is revealed here), today he is a well-rounded personality who spends his time raising money for local charities, including St. Luke's. So if you are in Sheffield and you see a small guy in a flat cap and muffler, playing a barrel organ for charity, do stop and say hello.

Gerry Allerston

CHAPTER 1

WAIFS AND STRAYS

I was born on 9 July 1933 in what was City General Hospital, now the Northern General, but my address was given as 55 Garden Street, off Broad Lane.

My first memories of life are of when I was just a few months old. Some people don't believe it's possible to remember so early but I can, and though they are only fragments, they are very clear in my mind. They are of a backyard, rough and gravelly. I am sat on the ground, just able to sit up without falling over, and my mother is pegging out some washing onto a line stretched across from an old house to some outbuildings. There is another woman doing the same. I am crying to be picked up, holding my arms out towards my mother and trying to shuffle on my bum to her, but she takes no notice of me. I also remember that the house had wooden shutters outside, which were closed at night with an iron bolt put through from the outside and a nut and washer put on the inside. Years later when I was out tatting with my dad (tatters were rag men who went out tatting with a horse and cart, collecting rags and other tat, and sometimes the horse would pull a bam box, which was a large barrow with wringer-machine handles for wheels), we would sometimes go up Garden Street as a short cut. All the old houses had been demolished, but at the top of this very steep hill we'd stop to give the pony a breather, and my dad would point to a stone step which was all that was left of this particular house and say, 'Tha' were our front step.' Nothing more, then we'd move on.

My mother used to tell of how, often, people would jump off Ball Bridge into the River Don to commit suicide, and they would be pulled out of the river at Lady's Bridge. Or they would put their head in the gas oven. She said it was common for fights to break out on Saturday nights and for cellar grates to be thrown through front room windows.

Another story she told was that of her grandfather, on her father's side, a man called Richard Paget, born in 1860. He was a coal merchant at the age of 21 and in late 1881 he married an Emma White of Cromwell Street, Walkley. They had three sons: Henry, Samuel and Albert and they lived at 43 Howard Street (just above the railway station). But one day in the early 1890s, Richard Paget left the house in the morning, as usual, and they never saw him again, and when they did eventually hear from him, he was in Philadelphia, USA. Whatever he had been pursuing, he must have been very successful in his endeavours because when her father was still a young boy, Richard Paget sent a man from Philadelphia to get the three boys and take them back with him to the USA. The story goes that when the man got to the port (Liverpool or Southampton) and was ready to embark, the youngest boy started to cry to go home. This man told my mother's father who, I think, would have been around 10 to 12 years old, 'I'm going to put you back on the train to take him home to Sheffield,' and the man then took the middle son, Samuel, to Philadelphia. When the two brothers got back to Sheffield, their mother put the younger son, Albert, into a boys' home so that Richard couldn't try it a second time. She didn't send Henry to the home because she considered him too old.

Henry Alfred Paget, who was born in 1882, went on to have four daughters, one of whom was my mother. I understand that Richard Paget corresponded with his two sons in Sheffield in the early 1920s, his last letter saying he was going to Miami for six months.

It seems his success came from pool halls and oyster bars, amongst other ventures, and whilst he appears to have been very prosperous, he also looks to be a very hard man.

My mother was a good storyteller. She grew up in Dun Street off Shalesmoor, now part of Kelham Island, and used to talk about her life as a young girl. My dad never talked much about his life, but my mother told us that when he was a little boy, he was in plaster from his ankles to his waist for two years, probably because he had rickets, which was very common then, and often resulted in bow legs. She said my grandfather George Edward Naylor was a bully and that his four sons, when they had become old enough, had planned to wait for him to come in one night and give him a good hiding: one son waited on the stairs, another at the top of the cellar steps and the other two in the kitchen, but when he came in, their nerves broke and they didn't carry it out. I have a strong recollection of my grandfather because though I saw him regularly, he never spoke a single word to me or my brother Terrence.

My father played the accordion, selling the instrument when he needed money and then buying another when he could afford it, and I remember that he had a very good voice and loved to sing, especially after a couple of pints. It turned out that his mother, who was Irish, had been a professional singer and half of a duo that sang in the music halls, including Sheffield Empire, under the name of O'Connor and Brady. She died in March 1934.

Garden Street was the first home my mother had after getting married. It was 2s/10d per week rent and my dad was only getting 17/6 labour money. Before that they'd lived in various rooms all around St. Philip's Road and parts of Upperthorpe, and she said to get the Garden Street house she had to pay 30 shillings key money and also let a man called Bill Green stay on as a lodger. He had one leg, the other being a wooden peg leg, and he used a wooden crutch. I think he lost his leg in the First World War, and I vaguely remember him coming to our house a few times after we'd moved onto the Wybourn, but my mother and father had lots of friends and our house was always full.

My mother had three sisters and four stepsisters. Her mother had worked in a brickyard up Rutland Road and my mother said she remembered how, when she was little, she often saw her mother lying still on an old settee. She died from consumption when my mother was about five years old and, soon afterwards, her father married again. The story was that one night there was a knock on the door and when her father opened it, there was a young woman stood there holding a little baby girl. She had been lodging in a house in the same yard but had been turned out and had come to ask if she could stay for the night, so he let her in. Her name was Annie Streets and so was the baby's. He married her soon after and I think he would have done it to have a mother to his own daughters. He had a further three daughters to Annie, the youngest, Betty, being just five weeks older than myself.

Richard Paget with son Samuel

Far right – Richard Paget's eldest son
Henry Alfred Paget (born 1882) on a Sunday outing

My paternal grandmother – the music hall singer (photo taken 1890s)

My father aged two and a half with his sister Agnes

CHAPTER 2

EARLY DAYS

When I was two-and-a-half-years old, my mother had a second baby boy, Terrence, born in January 1936. I recall that she had asked me one night if I would like a little sister or a little brother, but I don't remember what my reply was. (I just remember going home by tram, getting off at the bottom of Manor Lane and that one of my dad's friends carried me up. But something must have changed as the next time we were going up Manor Lane and I was wanting to be carried I was told no, so I had to walk. And crying made no difference.) Around that time, one Sunday morning, I got up and went downstairs to where one of my mother's sisters had just lit the fire. She had put the coal shovel and a sheet of newspaper across the fire to make it draw, and I pushed a chair right in front of the fire and climbed onto it. Suddenly, there was a loud crack and a red-hot coke shot out and hit me straight between the legs, burning through my pyjamas and sticking to my little willie. The rest is just a blur but for some time after my mother was putting ointment on it and bandaging it up before I went to bed, reminding me of how, when she had just had me, she would put a big napkin on me at bedtime in case I marked the bed.

As I have said, our house was always full with my mam and my dad's family and friends staying at weekends, and they would have a party at the slightest excuse. My father liked a drink and always finished up "merry", and my mother used to say that when they got married, they had a barrel of beer and a good time was had by all. Anyhow, one particular weekend they'd had a good Saturday night and some of the revellers stayed the night, the women going up to bed and the men sleeping downstairs, my father on the settee. The fire had been banked up to keep the house warm. The next morning everyone got up and my mother was in the kitchen cooking breakfast while her sister Connie was clearing out the ashes and relighting the fire because it had gone out. As she was doing so, she called out to my mother that there was an awful smell coming from the grate and the ashes. My mother came in from the kitchen and said straight away that she knew why that was and rounding sharply on my dad, said, 'Ah know wha's 'appened, you dirty fuckin' so and so!' He had got up from the settee in the night, still drunk, and pissed the fire out.

On quieter evenings my brother Terrence and me would sit on the peg rug in front of the fire, and a neighbour who we called Aunt Nell used to come round to our house, always about seven to eight o'clock, and wash the pots for my mother, and then they would sit and talk about the old days. I think my mother and Nell met when they both lived in Garden Street before my parents were re-housed at 62 Southend Place on the new Wybourn estate in the 1930s as part of a slum clearance scheme. Many years later Terrence bought that house (which my mother loved) under the Right to Buy Scheme and modernised it for her and my father to live in rent free until they died. Sadly, Terrence died before them and my mother tried to claim the house as hers, saying my brother meant her to have it as a gift. His widow had to take her to court over it. My mother lost and had to start paying rent to my brother's wife.

Aunt Nell was married to an Irish navvy, a quiet, gentle man named Jim Mulryan who, I believe, died some time before Nell. She was a lovely and loving woman and like a second mother to my mother, as well as us kids. At Christmas, when my mother went for a drink with my dad, Aunt Nell would baby-sit us, asking only for a tin of snuff in return.

Over time, things changed and got quieter but whenever one of my mother's sisters had a problem, they knew who to turn to for help as my mother was a doer rather than a "tea and sympathy" type. Quite often, when my mother and father went out for a drink at the weekend, they would go to the places and pubs they were familiar with in Upperthorpe, Shalesmoor and Meadow Street, and if they met someone down on their luck with nowhere to sleep, they would bring them back to sleep on the settee and have breakfast the next morning. That's how they met an old man who became a friend and came to our house for some years after. We called him Gran though his real name was Brunt and, gradually, he spent more time at our house than he did his own. He was a very knowledgeable man, especially about herbs, and in those days people more often visited an herbalist than a chemist or a doctor. Gran lived in Attercliffe, and I think he had served in the First World War as he used to talk about it sometimes. Now and then when he came to our house he would stay the night, sleeping on an old horsehair settee. Some weekends when my mam and dad would go out for a drink, Gran would baby-sit me and my brother. I was about four years old and my brother Terrence about two. To keep us amused Gran would let us shave him. I would get a cup of soapy water and my dad's safety razor and lather brush while he sat on the edge of an old wooden kitchen chair. I would stand behind him on the chair and shave his neck and the sides of his face, over and over again. Then my brother would try to have a go but, by this time, Gran's face was as smooth as a baby's bottom and shining.

Times were hard for my mother and I remember her walking from 62 Southend Place, Wybourn to the house of her sister Annie Paget at the bottom of Henry Street/Infirmary Road. When my brother was just a few months old, he was in an old-fashioned pram with big wheels and it had something like a well in the bottom where she put a bottle for him. I had to hold onto the pram handle, running to keep up as she always walked fast. We must have walked (or in my case run) all the way from the Wybourn because it was a big pram and no way could she have got it onto a bus, and I remember walking on Bank Street and Queen Street. We used to go regularly to her sister's (Annie) and I would play outside on the front, going as far as the infirmary gates, where I remember an Italian woman used to stand with an ice-cream barrow. Later on I learned her name was Toni and she lived in Southend Road, which was two minutes from our house.

When I was four, my dad bought me some wheels of my own, a second-hand three-wheeled bike with pump up tyres. He got it off someone who lived next door to my granddad in Shirecliffe and I clearly remember my dad tying a long piece of rope to the front of the bike and pulling me all the way from Shirecliffe to the Wybourn. I didn't have it very long. I was out playing on it when a bigger kid took it off me to have a ride and crashed it into some railings and buckled one of the wheels. My dad took it away from me and put it upstairs and I don't know what happened to it.

When I was five years old, my mother had another baby, a girl. She was named Brenda and was born at home on 23 July 1938. When it was time, I had to run and fetch Mrs Burgess (Connie), a neighbour who lived at the opposite end of our block of four houses, as my mother had asked her to look after her during her confinement, as they called it then (she always had Mrs Burgess) and Mrs Burgess then sent for the midwife. As this was during the day, my dad was out so there was just me and my brother Terrence. My mother was in bed and Mrs Burgess was up and down the stairs every few minutes. Terrence and me were sat at the bottom of the stairs and I had my arm round his shoulder, holding him close to me – my mother was screaming her head off and we were frightened to death. Eventually Mrs Burgess came and said, 'Tha's got a little sister.' I don't remember seeing my dad; I don't know where he'd got to.

The following January or February, when my sister was six or seven months old, my mother got a job at a cutlery firm called Sipples Ltd. on Blast Lane (at the bottom of Broad Street) as a spoon and fork dollier. It was a Saturday morning and she had to go to work – Saturday was half-day working – and Gran was to come to our house to look after us. This Saturday morning she was all ready for work but he hadn't come so, finally, she said to me, even though I was only just five years old, 'Ah've got to get off. Gran won't be long so ah want tha to look after these two till 'e comes. Tha'll be alright.' And off she went. By about an hour later I knew he wasn't coming and it was down to me, so I had to do what I'd seen my mother do. I got my brother dressed, got a soapy flannel and washed his hands and face and did the same for my sister. We had an old pushchair which I put outside the back door. Then I got my sister, wrapped her in a blanket and carried her outside and strapped her into the pushchair. I also did my best to clean the house up, including washing the floor. But then it started to rain so I went outside to fetch my sister in. There were three steps to our back door and I had the pull the pushchair up them. Well, I got it up the first step but couldn't get it up the others. I never thought to take her out of the pushchair. I decided to try the front door, went round and opened it, and wheeled her down the path. Again, I got her up the first step but, try as I might, I wasn't strong enough to get her and the pushchair any further. By now it was raining faster and I was trying all ways but just couldn't do it. I started to panic. Just at that moment, the next-door neighbour, a lady called Mrs Hutton, came out. Seeing what was happening, she lifted up the back of the pushchair for me whilst I lifted the front and we got my sister into the house. My mother came home at dinner time and learned that Gran hadn't come and we'd been on our own. She was very upset but full of praise for me. Later that week, when the insurance collector came (a man called Mr Richardson), she told him how I'd looked after the other two and, telling me how well I'd done, he gave me a silver sixpence.

As the eldest I had to help look after my brother Terrence and sister Brenda, who used to cry after me when I went to school. By the time I was seven or eight years old I knew how to make up a baby's bottle (usually a medicine bottle) with Ostermilk powder and feed them and wind them, and when my mam and dad went for a drink at the weekends, I'd see to the others and then get them off to sleep.

During these early years my father usually had his own horse and cart. One particular Sunday he had gone down to the stable, which was in South Street Park near The Sun Inn, to feed the horse and brush it down. Whilst he was brushing its flank, it swung its head round and bit him on the back of his head, nearly scalping him. By the time he'd made his way to a doctor living on City Road who put the skin and scalp back in place and stitched it down, the back of my father's neck, shirt and coat were covered in dried blood. He didn't go back to the doctor, much less the hospital; however, the next day he went to the stable and nearly killed the horse. Then he sold it.

Another time when my mother was in a story-telling mood, she told us about when they'd just got married and my dad was sent to prison for seven days for not paying a £5 fine. She went round trying to borrow the money to pay the fine and when she finally got it, went down to the charge office to pay. The policeman there said to her, 'Look, love, 'e's already done two days an' 'e'll not be out while tomorrow so 'e'll 'ave done three days out of the seven. Is it worth it?' So she didn't pay the fine and by letting him finish the seven days, instead, she had saved £5. (I don't know what he said when he got to know.) But he said that whilst he was in prison, he had to scrub a stone-flagged corridor and the prison warder would kick the bucket over and tell him to do it again.

I also remember that whenever it got near my parents' wedding anniversary, she would start reminding my dad and be saying how long they'd been married, but he never took any notice. I never knew him to buy anyone a greeting card, or wish anyone happy birthday or merry Christmas. I never heard him tell a joke or laugh at one, or say please or thank you. I never saw him take a drink of water, only beer. Though he did enjoy a game of snooker and I believe he was pretty good at it when he was younger.

My mother at about 25 years of age (about 1938)

CHAPTER 3

MY DAD THE ENTREPRENEUR

My father had gone out early. I don't know what day of the week it was but my mother was cleaning up when my father came back in, all of a rush. He had a folded newspaper in the side pocket of his coat; we didn't have a wireless and he'd been down town to get the latest news. He was all excited and saying to my mother over and over again, 'Th' is a war on! War's been declared! Th' is a war on wi' Germany!' It was scary. Until that minute, I didn't even know there were any other countries in the world besides ours.

To give the reader some idea of what life was like at 62 Southend Place and that it was never dull, I recall the following: In Boundary Road (number 47, I think) there lived a family called the Wards, who I came to know quite well but whom my parents already knew very well. There was Mr and Mrs Ward, I think Mr Ward had just started his own demolition firm, and they had quite a large family: five sons and two daughters, the eldest child being a son called Tommy. From what my mother used to say, he would have been in his early twenties and in the army and, at this time, home on leave. Mr and Mrs Ward and Tommy had gone into town for a drink. At the end of the evening they had gone back home and continued an argument which had started earlier. Matters had got ugly and ended with Mr Ward hitting Tommy on the head with a poker. Tommy ran out, straight across the gardens to our house, and I remember standing in the kitchen, watching my dad bathing Tommy's head and blood running down Tommy's face and neck. He didn't go back at the end of his leave, and eventually the police went to Mr and Mrs Ward's house looking for Tommy, saying he was a deserter. Of course, the Wards sent the police to our house and my dad said that Tommy had been there and went on to tell them what had happened. The police said they would have to search the house. They did, but didn't find him. After they had gone (much to my mam and dad's relief), all my parents could say was, 'It's a fuckin' good job they didn't look int' loft!' I understand that Tommy went back soon afterwards. My mam and dad remained good friends with Mr and Mrs Ward, and I think my dad worked for Mr Ward but it only lasted a few weeks. Mr Ward died two or three years later.

Every house in our street was given an air-raid shelter, and we had to dig a big hole in the back garden to put the shelter in after putting it together, of course. We also got some wooden bunks for sleeping on. The shelters were great places for the kids to play, but soon the air-raids started and they became so regular that some people used to put their kids in the shelter to sleep in for the whole night. On the night of the Sheffield Blitz, Thursday 12 December 1940, everybody went into their shelters early, my mother making sure we all had our gas masks. My sister was in something like a big rubber container and my brother Terrence had a mask that was red and a bit like a Mickey Mouse face. The bombs dropped left, right and centre and they seemed to be getting closer and closer, but my dad was in and out of the shelter each time there seemed to be a bit of a lull and my mother kept shouting at him to come inside. Me and my brother were sat on the bottom bunk, either side of my mother.

She had her arms around both of us, squeezing us to her. It was pitch-black inside the shelter, and every time a bomb landed the ground shook, and we could here the slates coming of the roofs. The nearest bomb landed about 100 yards away on Boundary Road – you could have easily buried a double-decker bus in the crater! Gradually, everything went quiet and eventually it started to come daylight. My mam and dad left the shelter and went into our house to look around. They came back saying, 'We can't stay 'ere.' All the doors were blown off and all the windows blown out plus other damage so we set off walking. They didn't say where we were going and, at that moment, I'm not sure they knew themselves. We walked down to the bottom of Wybourn, down Woodburn Road to Attercliffe where Gran Brunt lived on Newhall Road. We got a cup of tea, but me and another kid had to go to the fire station to get a bucket of water first. From there we walked to my mother's sister's house, which was number 82 Deerlands Avenue, Parson Cross. They took us in but there was already another family there (on her husband's side), so there were three families, including seven kids, and we were all in their shelter on the Sunday night when Sheffield was raided again. Finally, on the Tuesday morning, my mother said to me and my brother, 'Come on, get ready, we're goin' 'ome.' So we set off to walk back to the Wybourn – and it was a very long walk – where we all set-to clearing up the mess as best we could. However, a few days later my dad found out that the government was paying compensation to anyone who had bomb damage to their house, so he went upstairs and made a hole in the bedroom ceiling and started a small fire to scorch some of the floor boards and then made a claim for fire damage. No-one ever came to check and he got just over £14 to cover the damage.

After the main air-raid, we were still having ordinary raids. Some of the ARP men were fire watchers and a group was formed for the top of Wybourn, where they had a post on the roof of The Windsor Hotel; from here they could see right across the roofs of all the houses and would have seen any fires immediately. Two men in charge of organising this came to our house and I remember the occasion when they told my dad he should take a turn at fire watching. He looked at them and then pointed to the fire in the grate, saying, 'Tha's the only fire ah'm watchin'!' Eventually they stopped coming, but when someone asked him if he was going to join the army he said, 'T'only army ah'm joinin' is Salvation Army.'

The authorities were calling up men from different age groups for medical checks to see if they were fit for service. My father had to go despite not being in the best of health and my mother was really worried (on the day, she was like a cat on hot bricks). He got back mid-afternoon and the instant he walked into the kitchen she jumped on him, almost shouting, "ow's tha gone on?' 'Grade four,' he said, meaning his health wasn't good at all and so he wasn't fit for the army. All she could say was, 'Thank fuck for that,' never thinking there might be something seriously wrong with him. And that was that. We were back to normal.

Soon after this there was an accident in the kitchen. The means of cooking was limited to a copper boiler with a gas tap on the wall, and above it, on top of the boiler, stood a gas ring with a rubber tube to the gas tap. On this gas ring my mother would boil the kettle or a saucepan for potatoes, etc. One night she was boiling a saucepan of water when my sister Brenda, aged about two, wandered into the kitchen whilst my mother was at the sink. No-one saw her reach up and touch the saucepan handle; the pan came off the gas ring and the boiling water spilled onto the floor and onto my sister's feet. She screamed out and my mother did everything she could think of but very quickly my sister's feet became covered in huge blisters. My mother ran up to the doctor's surgery (Dr Jacobs) in Manor Lane and he came and took charge. My mam and dad brought a bed downstairs, and the doctor gave my mother a spray of some liquid for Brenda's feet. She used to scream in pain every time it was applied. After about a week the blisters formed hard, black crusts and two or three weeks later these began peeling off, leaving new skin and no scars. Happily, she doesn't remember any of this.

Also around this time, my mother's youngest sister, Connie, had been staying with us. She was pregnant and her husband, Jim Coppley, was in the army, so as she was on her own, my mother brought Connie to stay with us until the baby was born, which was during one of the air-raids. To make it easier on my mother, me and my brother had been spending nights at a neighbour's in Southend Road. They were a big family with a lot of kids, perhaps eight or nine, and they had a double-size shelter. Eventually, because the house wasn't big enough – her father and cousin also lived with them – they exchanged the house and went to live in a bigger one on Attercliffe Common. The woman, Mrs Gurnhill, ended up having about sixteen kids, though some of them died fairly young, including her eldest son, Edward, when he was 16 or 17 and a good pal of mine. He had just started working down the pit, and a detonator exploded close to him. He died from a brain tumour started, his parents believe, by the detonator.

During the earlier years of the war, one way or another, I think we

19

lived better than most and though there were difficulties, it was during these times that my mother was at her best. She was always quick to learn of anything to be had for us from any charity, church or the school and nowhere was too far for her to go for it. My dad always felt intimidated by officialdom but not her, she was like a terrier with a rat and would argue or cajole until she got something for us. I knew what it was to have bread and dripping or bread and jam for my breakfast or dinner and throughout those early years me and my brother had plenty of it, but we never went to bed hungry like lots of kids I knew. (Once, when we had two pennyworth of chips each for our dinner, Terrence cut every chip down the middle before making them into chip sandwiches as that way he had ten slices of bread off a sliced loaf.)

My father always managed to scrape some money together, and at one time we had a big hut in our back garden where we kept a lot of ducks and hens, so people were always coming to ask if we had eggs to sell. Of course we had, but my father always charged top prices and as soon as the laying slowed down, he would sell the birds off. Someone used to come with an old lorry and a load of crates and we would catch all the birds, put them in the crates, and off they went. He would then buy another lot of ducks and hens and start again. But everyone on the Wybourn knew my dad and when someone wanted something they knew to see Lol Naylor, no matter what it was – petrol coupons, a piece of pork, furniture, suits and dresses, anything – my father would know someone. A couple of years after the war had ended we were building some pig styes on Hyde Park, near the dog track. I was 14.. My dad's brother-in-law Arnold Whittington, who had just come out of the Navy, was doing the bricklaying. (Everyone used to call him Dick and ask where his cat was.) He was up on some old scaffolding and I was labouring for him and talking about my dad being able to get anything for anyone when Arnold became very angry. He stopped working and looked at me for a few seconds before saying, and his exact words were, 'Thi father! Thi father! ... Thi father were a fuckin' spiv!' I didn't say anything but I thought about it and said to myself, he's right. He was, and I felt a little proud of my dad.

Me and my brother Terrence (or Tets as a lot of the kids called him) were always fighting or wrestling each other. I think we were contending for "top dog". My mother used to get fed up with it and we'd get a good hiding but I got it the worst because I was the older. Once he locked me out of the house, knowing I had to clean up before my mother got home, and I finished up getting so mad I put my fist through a window to get in, so then I got a double good hiding. But we would always stick up for each other against anyone else. When were older, a kid called Ronnie Cox had been hitting my brother in the street. He'd done it a few times and he was bigger than our Tets, so this Sunday teatime I was going down the street as he was coming up and without thinking I chased him, caught him and gave him a taste of his own medicine, even though I was pals with his brother. The whole street came out and somebody ran and fetched his father but by this time it was too late. However, he learnt his lesson and never hit my brother again. In those days I always got in first and would let rip without even thinking about it and, of course, all the other kids loved to see a fight and would egg you on. That's how it was.

During the war years my mother was just as enterprising as my dad and, on the whole, we had more than our fair share of what was going. Periodically my mother would draw the rations early (on a ration book) and then write me a note to take to the Food Office on West Street to say that we had lost a ration book. They would give me what were called emergency coupons for the same week so we got double rations that week and also a new book shortly afterwards.

There were other times when money was very scarce and things were hard, but my mother had two rules by which she lived: always pay your rent, and keep a good fire – then it doesn't matter if you've had the light cut off (which happened more than once and she always had candles in the cupboard, just in case). One day when my dad had been out tatting, he came home a bit earlier than usual, all flustered and agitated. He said that he had been going down Broad Street with the pony and cart, and as he went past the bottom of Duke Street and on towards Sheaf Street, who should be standing on the pavement waiting to cross the road? – the Relief Inspector who had been to our house many times. My father rode right past him and, fortunately, the pony was running. All my dad could say was, "'e's seen me, 'e's fuckin' seen me!' As my dad was on the relief at the time, this was serious. When he told my mother she said he might not have but if he had, 'Tha will jus' 'ave to stick it out, won't tha!' As luck would have it nothing came of it, perhaps because my dad passed him too fast or maybe the man was preoccupied as he stood there.

By this time, I was having time off school to help my dad with whatever he was doing – hawking, tatting – anything with a horse and cart. When I was six or seven my dad would have been into

Castlefolds Wholesale Fruit and Vegetable Market, which was situated behind what is now Wilkinson, in Haymarket/Dixon Lane. Whatever he had bought, for example: flowers, fruit, celery, etc., I would have to take round every house in Southend Place, or he would put together a bunch of radishes, lettuce and two tomatoes, which were very scarce, and tell me to go and ask Mrs so-and-so if she wanted a nice salad for a shilling. So I'd go to every house doing this and two out of every three would buy, but the tomatoes were a sprat to catch a mackerel and sometimes someone would say, 'Ah don't want the salad, but tell thi dad ah'll 'ave some tomatoes.' When I told him this, he would say, 'Tell 'er to fuck off.'

My dad was always thinking of ways to make money and some of them were bizarre. Gran, being very knowledgeable about herbs and potions, suggested making beer, that is, milk stout. So my dad bought all the ingredients – hops, liquorice and other things – and made gallons of the stuff using the kitchen boiler. The end result meant that there were gallons of milk stout around the house in bowls, jugs and various containers. But he'd forgotten about bottles so we all drank as much as we could, while my mother was playing hell as she wanted her saucepans and things back. I don't know what he did with the rest as I don't think he sold much of it.

After that, as women did all the laundry, Gran suggested that my dad make a liquid for getting clothes clean. Again, he bought all the ingredients – soft soap, ammonia and whatever else – and boiled them all together in the kitchen boiler. And this time he collected some bottles. When the stuff got going it started to give off a lot of fumes, and I can still picture him now, stood in the kitchen with a gas mask on, stirring it up with a brush handle. We had the kitchen door closed but the fumes were coming under the door so my mother put a towel down to keep them out. Once again she was playing hell with my father, this time because us kids and her were sat on the settee with tears streaming down our faces. But this liquid soap turned out to be something of a success; it was very good for getting clothes clean and he sold it all! The trouble was it cost more to make than he could sell it for.

In addition to all this, we were still going out hawking and tatting, doing chimney-sweeping and anything else that came along. My dad started cleaning windows but I was too little and too young to help with this, though I do remember a woman called Lily Allen working for him – she did the bottoms while he did the tops. He charged 7d and 10d for two- and three-bedroomed houses. While he was tatting, he was also selling pots (crockery) as well as giving them away for rags. At this time, we were still having air-raids. He was stabling the horse in a yard in Samson Street, which is off Duke Street, below the Park Library, and he kept his pots there in baskets. He went one morning after a raid to find that there was damage to the roof, and the bricks and slates had come down and smashed most of his pots. I had to go round the local streets, door-to-door, selling what was left.

My mother and Brenda at Southend Place (1939-40)

CHAPTER 4

THE PIKELET MAN

During these years, times were really hard and uncertain. My mother was never sure whether or not she was going to get any housekeeping money off my dad and, if so, how much or when. He used to leave her what he could on a daily basis when he left the house, which was usually about 9 am. If she complained, 'Tha's not enough!' his reply was always the same: 'Ah've gen tha what ah've got,' and then there would be a row. Although she was a marvel at making it go as far as it did, sometimes it would get on top of her, but my dad never concerned himself with such mundane things as how the next rent would get paid or any other bills, those were my mother's problems. One particular morning he'd left her what he'd got, on the table, and was just going out the back door when she saw how much it was, just half-a-crown instead of the hoped for 4 shillings. She went mad, cursing and swearing and all he would say was, 'Tha's all ah've got.' Then he left the house and I've remembered all my life what she shouted after him: 'Ah 'ope tha gets run o'er wi' fuckin' bus!' And even though I must only have been about nine years old, I went cold as something flashed across my mind: one day she will say that to me. And then, as he walked down the path, she opened the window and threw the half-crown at him. Nevertheless, we still had a hot tea that night and I can honestly say we used to have a hot tea every night except Saturdays, a cooked breakfast every Sunday morning and, always, a really good Sunday dinner. My mother was a marvellous cook and anyone who was in the house at the time would have a plate put out for them and they would have the same as us. So there were times when my mother seemed to have a heart of stone and other times just the opposite and two particular instances of this come to mind.

Every few weeks during the summer, usually at about 10 - 10.30 a.m., an old man used to come into our street (actually, it was known as a keyhole). Today such a man would be regarded as a tramp – old overcoat, flat cap, unshaven and down-at-heel. He would stand in the middle of the street, take off his cap and start to sing, usually three or four songs. Some of the windows would open and he would then go from window to window, holding out his cap, and people would put in a copper or two. Every time, my mother would open the window and beckon for him to come across. He knew what she meant because she always did the same thing. She would say to me, 'Tek 'im this.' Always the same, two thick slices of bread and dripping and a pint of tea plus two pennies and he would sit on our front step to have it. (As I write this, I feel fondness at this memory, the kinder side to her.)

Quite often, by the middle of the week she would be counting her coppers up to put a hot tea together and would get any bottles that had a deposit on them, some 1d, others 2d, and all together she might have a shilling or 1/6. If I had 3d or 6d from running errands, she would say, 'Lend it me.' Actually, I didn't have a choice. She would write on a scrap of paper with a little stump of a pencil, which she always had on her, a list of say: 6 pennyworth of potatoes, half a turnip, 6 pennyworth of carrots and whatever else she needed, for me to take to the shop, saying only, 'Co-op.' Other times, she would send me across the road to a Mrs Boardman's house.

Now, Mrs Boardman was an old woman with what everyone regarded as a "good carry on". One son was a miner so she got half a ton of coal every few weeks, and two other sons worked for her son-in-law, who was building up a very substantial business as a coal merchant and a little later on as a demolition contractor. His name was Jimmy Childs (of James Childs Ltd.) He had a huge yard in Manor Lane where he stored reclaimed timbers and other materials. During the week there would be a constant stream of people with barrows going up to Childs' yard to buy logs and firewood. When I was eight or nine and wanted to earn something for myself, I would first have to finish whatever work I had been told to do, but I always tried to have a few coppers of my own in my pocket, so when I'd finished my work, I would borrow a barrow off someone and go up to Jimmy Childs' yard. There, I'd buy 6d worth of wood, sometimes a shilling's worth, chop it up into sticks and then make it up into bundles of firewood to sell at 3d a bundle. In time, Jimmy became something of a godfather figure on the top of Wybourn; if anyone who lived on the Wybourn was out of work or down on their luck and went to see Jimmy for a job, they always got set on.

One particular day, my mother sent me across to ask Mrs Boardman if she could lend her 4 shillings. This was standard routine, the rule being: at the shop you had to give Mrs Boardman's Co-op number so she would get the "divi". She got her purse and gave me half-a-crown, saying, 'Tell thi mother tha's all ah've got.' So I went back home and my mother gave me her list. Off I went to the shops (I think I was eight) and I remember it was a miserable day. I know I was dawdling, walking on the edge of the path without stepping on a line, the half-crown in my hand. Then disaster struck – the half-crown slipped out of my hand just as I was walking over a grate in the road. It was gone. I tried to look through the slots in the grate but it was just a big black hole. Soon enough I knew I had to go back and tell my mother that I had lost the money, and I was petrified. I knew what was coming but I went into the house and I told her. I got good hidings regularly, perhaps every one or two weeks, and when we went to live at 62 Southend Place (about 1934) she had a stair carpet put down which included a set of twelve wooden rods. Over the years she broke every one of them across my back. She made no secret of this, telling anyone who would listen, as if she were proud of it, and she used to say, 'The 'arder tha is the more they'll think on tha.' Well now she gave me the beating of my life, something special. She knocked me and kicked me from one room to another, hitting me with everything she could put her hand on. Then she pushed me out of the house, telling me quite calmly, 'Don't come back till tha's got that half-crown,' and she meant it.

I went back to the grate and tried to pull the lid up but there was no way as I was just too little and the grate was too heavy. But I knew I couldn't go back without that half-crown so in desperation I went to the house nearest the grate, which was the middle house in a block of four in Southend Road. (I knew everyone who lived in this road.) I knocked on the front door and a man came out. I managed to tell him what had happened and that I wanted him to get my half-crown out of the grate. I'll never know how I did explain this to him because he was deaf and dumb (everyone used to refer to him as "the dummy") but I did manage it. As a result, he came out, got the grate lid up, lay in the road on his stomach and got his hand and arm right down the hole. He fished around in the muck and filth and found my half-crown! So I was able to go home and then go to the shops.

Some days later, I was stood looking out of the window, which was all steamed up, and it was miserable and grey and raining. My mother was sat beside the fire and telling a friend about me losing the money. I was silent, seemingly just looking out but I was listening intently to what was being said. I had got over the hiding and was listening as if she done it to someone else when, suddenly, right at the end of the tale she said, 'Ah think ah went a bit too far.' Only when she said that did it affect me and whilst I made no sound, floods of tears ran down my face as I sobbed inwardly. She never knew how I felt, and the beatings didn't stop and I was never able to understand why she would be like this (the other side to her).

I have said that my mother was a good storyteller – stories about her life as a little girl, stories about what she knew about my dad and how they met. I was surprised to learn, years later, that my dad was born in the Park district, in South Street. He never spoke about where he was born and I had assumed it was somewhere around Upperthorpe way. But it seems that his family moved from the Park district to the Upperthorpe area, where they lived in Wentworth Street, Martin Street, Martin Lane and other streets. Sometimes when he'd had a drink and was a bit maudlin, he'd say he was born without a shirt to his back and his mother didn't have a blanket to wrap him in so 'Ah come int' t' world wi' nowt an' ah'll go out wi' nowt.'

As a young man, he used to go door-to-door selling kippers for 3d a pair. When my mother's family lived in Dun Street, my dad used to go all around that area with his kippers in a box that he carried on his head. Apparently, he became sweet on one of my mother's stepsisters, but she wouldn't go out with him because he had kipper oil running down the sides of his face and neck, so he rubbed the kipper oil into her hair and asked my mother out instead. They married when she was just 18 and he 22.

My mother used to talk about her family and especially her father. It was obvious that she had loved him very much. She said he never swore and didn't drink. She talked about how he would often go to work and not have any packing up for his dinner, so he would go for a walk round at dinner time so his mates wouldn't know he had no dinner. And she told us about how, when he got home from work, he would have to set-to and give them their tea, including his wife (her stepmother), who had no idea how to lay money out. I vaguely remember him. He was a bit on the bonny side and quiet, but he used to play with me. I remember swinging between his knees and him giving me a halfpenny to go to the Wall's "Stop Me and Buy One" for an orange Jubbly ice (a three sided lolly with no stick, that you had to push up from the bottom of its cardboard container).

Apart from watching every penny, my mother was obsessive about things being clean. (She had dermatitis on her hands from always using bleach to get clothes clean.) And she would always sing as she was cleaning. There was the morning ritual of raking out all the old ashes and then taking up the pegged rug and the coconut mats, one each side of the table, and shaking them out the back. Then put every last coke back and relight the fire, putting a shovel and the previous night's *Star* up in front to make it draw. All this time my mam would be singing: 'Pennies From Heaven', 'It's My Mother's Birthday Today', 'Little Pal', 'If Daddy Goes Away' and others, and she put such feeling into the songs it was as if she was in another world. I thought she had a beautiful and very powerful voice and I hung onto every word; I felt safe and secure. However, all that came to an end the day my mother's father died.

It was 1937. I was outside playing in the slop dosh (mud) with a spoon when my mother's two young stepsisters came running up the street. Olive was 14 years old and Gladys 10. My mother would have been about 34. They came up the path and into the kitchen, shouting and crying, 'Lil, me dad's dead! Lil, me dad's dead!' When my mother comprehended what they were saying, she screamed and screamed. It was terrible to hear. It seems he'd been working on nights, getting home to his wife at about 7 a.m. She had lit the fire, and he was sat in his chair when he suddenly fell back heavily, and that was it. He was only about 54 years old. I never heard my mother sing again.

As we grew older, me and my brother had to help with cleaning the house. Many times I've had to scrub the bedroom floors and the stairs. Every Wednesday I'd empty cupboards, scrub them out and put fresh newspaper on the shelves and then put everything back and on Thursdays I'd have to do the same with the pantry shelves. Other tasks were blackleading the Yorkshire range and I'd do the steps, front and back, and then donkey stone them. Sometimes my mother would buy me a comic for doing this, *Radio Fun* or *Film Fun*. She taught me how to make bread. I'd sieve the flour through a stocking to get the bran out because it made the bread look grey and my dad would go off on one and wouldn't eat it. He was always funny about what he would and wouldn't eat – it had to be good and set out nicely on the plate. But then, often, he would have a mouthful and turn his nose up at it. He never thought about how hard my mother had worked to put a meal on the table, and she would get really mad and then he'd know about it. (He once came in drunk on a Sunday afternoon. She threw a plate at him, he ducked and it hit his pal, who was behind him, and took a lump out of his arm.)

One thing in particular that I looked forward to in the colder months was when the pikelet man came round on Sunday afternoons. He wore a brown smock and knee-high leather gaiters and rode a grocer's bike (which had a stand so it didn't fall over) with a box on the front containing a wicker basket. He'd stop and ring a big brass bell, shouting, 'Oatcakes an' pikelets,' and we'd dash out and get some to toast in front of the fire for our tea. (Today's supermarket pikelets don't taste nearly as good.) It was a ritual and I loved it and it's the little things like this that people remember when they talk about "the old days".

As a very little boy, I always felt that my mother was very happy being married to my dad, that she loved him very much, even though they rowed and fought the way they did. (My dad always lost.) Always, when he went out of the house to work, she would ask him what time he would be back. He might say 5 o'clock or 6 o'clock but sometimes he seemed to forget and it would get to 10 o'clock and she always knew why: he would have called into the pub for a pint, one pint led to another and before he knew it, it would be getting on for closing time. When it got to about 9 o'clock she knew what had happened so she would be boiling mad and would say to me, 'Put bolt on back door an' lock front door.' About 10 o'clock there he would be, trying the back door, knocking and shouting, 'Open t'door!' She would tell him to go away, or words to that effect, so then he'd go to the front door, backwards and forwards, shouting, 'Let me in! Open this fuckin' door!' Eventually he'd be sat on the front step singing to himself. (But he never seemed to know the words.) By this time it might be midnight and he'd be sobering up a bit and I'd say to my mother, 'Shall ah let 'im in, mam?' Only after a while would she say, 'Tek bolt off,' and he would come in, trying to explain that he'd only had two glasses – always two glasses – while she was saying how she'd been worrying and wondering if something had happened to him, then give him his tea. On the other hand, if they'd had a really bad row, she would go for days refusing to speak to him, only talking to him through me. The routine went something like this:

'Tell 'im 'is tea's ont' table.'

'Dad, me mam says your tea's ont' table.'

'Tell her ah don't fuckin' want it.'

'Mam, me dad says he don't want it.'

'Then tell 'im he can go wi'out.'

'Dad, me mam says to go wi'out.'

'Tell 'er to eat it 'er fuckin' sen.'

'Mam, me dad says to eat it yoursen.'

Then, bang, she'd throw it on the fire. This could carry on for days but he always knew how to get round her, in the end. He would develop a pain in his stomach or chest, having to fight for his breath. After a bit, she would begin to get concerned and look for the rubbing oil, goose grease, go down to the chemist for Thermogene wool, Belladonna plasters. She would be close to tears and all else was forgotten. One time they had a bad row that went on all week. It was around teatime and my dad was sat in his easychair, back to the kitchen door, while my mam was stood at the sink peeling potatoes. They were arguing back and forth when my dad said something that really got to her. I don't remember what it was but having just started peeling this big potato, she left the sink, shoved the middle door wide open and threw the potato. As he was sat with his back to her, it hit him right in the back of his neck and it looked as if his head was going to come off. He couldn't move his head for about a fortnight after that.

Something that happened to me, though it rarely comes to mind, fortunately, occurred when I was 9 or 10 years old, at Southend Place. The gas meter was on a shelf above the back door. (You had to put a penny in the slot and turn a brass ring round.) The gas had run out whilst my mother was cooking the dinner, and she shouted me to put a penny in the meter. By now I was pretty strong and instead of getting a chair to stand on, I'd hold the penny between my teeth, jump up, and hanging onto the shelf with one arm, put the penny in the meter. But this time, as I jumped up, the penny slid to the back of my throat, and I was hanging there just gurgling. Luckily, as my mother yelled me to stop messing about, my dad realised there was something wrong, and he charged into the kitchen and knocked me down from the shelf. My mother came over and, with one either side of me, they turned me upside down and started thumping me on the back until the penny shot out. There was no doubt about it, they saved my life, thanks to my dad's quick thinking. Both were shaking and white faced but when we'd all recovered, my mother said, 'Put tha' penny int' gas,' and my dad said, 'An' this time, stand ont' fuckin' chair.' I didn't need telling.

CHAPTER 5

HORSES FOR COURSES

When we were out hawking or tatting, I had to shout round the streets, same as my dad, and it became second nature. One time we had been out all day, finishing up on the Shirecliffe estate. We used to get back to the rag shop for about 4 o'clock, in time to weigh-in. You always had to go through the rags carefully looking for "sellers". Because we had our own pony and cart (turnout), we could weigh-in at any of the rag merchants, of which there were quite a few. We used to go to one called Elliott's in West Bar green, where the police station is now situated. If you borrowed one of their turnouts, they charged you 4 shillings a day and they only paid 18 shillings per cwt for tats, and 6d per lb in weight for wool. You needed a lot of rags for a hundredweight and you had a good day if you weighed in for £2, including a bit of scrap. Anyway, we were sorting out and putting the tats in a double size sack when I came across a brand new pair of riding breeches. I put them by to take home with the sellers and when we got home, I slipped them upstairs and hid them away – my brother and me were still wearing short trousers, even though I was asking if I could have some long trousers. A few days later, after school, it was warm and all the kids were out and about at the bottom of the street. I went upstairs and put on the riding breeches and then crept out and was off down the street. These breeches were light fawn in colour and just the same as Russ Abbot wore in his TV show – right baggy at the sides, like pantaloons, and coming just down to the calves, with the socks pulled up over the bottoms. I thought they were smashing but when the kids saw me, they all shouted, 'Where's thi 'orse?' My mother looked out of the window, and then was straight out onto the front step. She went mad, shouting me at the top of her voice, 'Get in this 'ouse and get 'em off!' However, she did go across to the school to see the headmistress and she got a note from her to take to the Welfare Centre at Manor Top where they had used clothing that was sent over from America. She took me and my brother, I think she was allowed two items for each of us, and I got a pair of long trousers just like Rupert Bear's – orange and brown check, and I got a jersey. (My brother didn't get any long trousers as she made him carry on wearing short ones until they wore out.) Back at school, when it was break time, all us lads went to the toilets where the others crowded around me because they'd never seen trousers before that had a zip on the fly instead of buttons.

I had started at Manor Lane School when I was four and a half. My mother took me for the first few days and after that I had to find my own way. A few months later, St. Oswald's Catholic School opened in Southend Road and she took me across and got me in there. I remember that I was late on my first morning and I was late thereafter, right up until leaving, because I always had something to do before going to school. But if there was ever anything to be had, she was never too proud to get it for us. Every so often she would go across to St. Oswald's and ask the headmistress for a ticket for us. With this ticket we could go to Langton's shoe shop in the Wicker where, on presenting the ticket, we would get a new pair of boots each. Other times she would get a voucher for a jerkin each. And she didn't stop there, she persisted until she got us free dinners at school, which I used to enjoy.

In the days when we used to go home for our dinner, one day there was a knock at our front door and my mother, who was in the kitchen, shouted me to see who it was. I went to the door and there was a woman there who lived in Boundary Road, with two of her children who were only very young, around five or six. I knew her well by sight, as she did us. My mother shouted, 'Who is it?' and came to the door. The woman was known to everyone as "Little Annie", for obvious reasons. She was almost crying and said to my mother, 'Mrs Naylor, ah've come to ask if tha could give me kids a bit of bread an' jam. They've 'ad no breakfast, ah've nowt to give 'em for dinner, an' I don't know what I can give 'em at teatime.' Without any hesitation, my mother simply said, 'My kids are only 'avin' bread 'n' drippin' but thi's more than welcome to come in an' 'ave same.' They did. And she made sure the bread slices were thick ones with a mug of tea to wash them down. Again, my mother showed her other side and I've never forgotten that day; I was so proud of her, and I had the greatest respect for that woman for not being too proud to put her kids' hunger before her pride.

The war was well underway. By now, Gran Brunt had a son called Charlie whose wife had died, and his little son was living with his grandparents. Charlie was working at a firm called Sanderson & Newbould, a steelworks on Newhall Road, Attercliffe. It came about that he had nowhere to live, so my mother took him in as a lodger. A few months later he told her about a workmate, Fred Widdowson (a quiet, inoffensive man who had a harelip and talked down his nose), who was in lodgings somewhere in Heeley, and she took him in as a lodger too. My mother charged them 30 /- each, per week, and they slept in the back bedroom. My brother and I shared a single bed in the front bedroom while my little sister, Brenda, slept in my parent's bed, in between them. So by this time there were four adults and three kids in a two-bedroomed council house. Charlie and Fred were getting good hot meals and everything done for them, and my mother could rely on a regular £3 a week, which made a huge difference to her housekeeping. When Fred moved in, my mother asked him where his belongings were. He told her he had been up to his old lodgings for them and the landlord refused to let him have them. This made my mother mad. She said, 'Right, we'll see about that, ah'll sort 'im out,' and a couple of days later she and a friend went up Heeley to ask the landlord for Fred's clothes and other belongings. He told her she wasn't getting them. So, with another 'We'll see about that,' she went to Woodseats police station, explained the situation and asked for their help. They sent a policeman with her to ask for Fred's belongings and the landlord told the policeman that she wasn't getting them. When the policeman insisted he hand them over, they started fighting in the house, and the man was arrested for assaulting a police officer. When it went to court, my mother was a witness. The man was sent down for 28 days, and Fred got his clothes and other belongings back. Afterwards, my mother went to where Fred's mother lived in Shiregreen. When she got back, she said that when talking about Fred, his mother told her that she'd had two sons but the other had recently been killed in France and that she wished it had been Fred, instead.

Charlie and Fred lived at our house for quite some time, and my mother put their board up to 35/- a week. Charlie, who used to go to the Windsor Hotel, finally married a barmaid who worked there, while Fred, who used to drink mostly in town at a pub called The Blue Boar on West Bar, married a woman who frequented the pub. My mother tried to talk him out of it, telling him that both the woman and her mother were known prostitutes but he still married her. Later on he told my mother that he wished he had listened to her but, by then, it was too late.

We were still tatting and hawking and over the years we must have had a dozen horses and carts, some of them good ones, some of them useless. At various times, we've stabled all over Sheffield: Well Road, Heeley; Bridgefield Road; Marcus Street, Pitsmoor; Hyde Park; behind Nunnery Colliery; Manor Lane and others, and early on Sunday mornings I would go down to the stable to fetch the pony out. Whilst we were keeping the pony up Pitsmoor, a bloke was sleeping in the stable on the bales of hay. (I thought it looked quite comfortable.) He was going out tatting with a barrow as well as doing a bit of singing in pubs, and he could yodel. His name was Gus and my dad must have felt sorry for him because he told him he could stretch out on our settee for a bit till he found somewhere to stay. My mother wasn't very keen on this idea and three or four days later she found out he had "a liking for kids". She went mad at my dad and said something like, 'Ah don't care a fuck where 'e sleeps. Tha'd better not bring 'im back tonight or tha'll be sleepin' int' fuckin' stable as well!'

One of the first times I had to fetch the pony and cart was up Pitsmoor. So this Sunday morning I eventually got there and got the pony harnessed up, though I had a job getting the collar over its head (I was about 9 or 10 at the time). I set off down Champs Hill, which is still there, and onto Stanley Street, Wicker. I got to where I had to cross to the other side so that I could go up the Wicker and then turn onto Blonk Street and on to the bottom of Broad Street. I stopped at the halt sign but then I lost my nerve at venturing out to cross to the other side, even though there was next to no traffic. In those days the railway had a lot of horses and drays – big shire horses and big, heavy drays, and mostly women drivers. I watched this woman driver come down the Wicker, go under the arches and disappear. About half an hour later I watched her come back up the other side towards Haymarket, as I was still trying to get up the nerve to cross the road. She saw me, looked across and then stopped her horse, which seemed huge (and it was). She got down and came across the road, and taking hold of my pony's bridle, said, 'Come on,' and took me across. Then giving me a smile, she returned to her own horse and off she went, and I continued on my way. (I never told my dad about it.)

It was summer time, and one of the things me and my dad would do in the summer, on a Saturday morning, was go round Castlefolds Wholesale Market at the last minute to buy a load of celery, perhaps twenty bundles, get it home and unload it on the yard. After the woman helped me across the road and I'd got back home, we all set-to cleaning and dressing the celery and setting it out on the cart. This took us till just after dinner time, so after we had a bite to eat, we set off round the estate – me, my brother and my dad. I worked the left-hand side of the street while my brother did the other, both of us going door-to-door, selling the celery at 4d and 6d a root. My dad worked from the cart, serving those who came out to select their own. We stayed out until about 4 o'clock, by which time people would be having their tea, so back home we binned anything we had left. It was my job to take the pony back and stable it, before which we would all turn our pockets out and count how much we had taken. Me and my brother would have about 35 shillings to £2 each but we never got to know how much my dad had taken.

One Sunday we went out with the celery and a kid about my age, called Titch Scott, asked my dad if he could he go with us. He said okay. Well, he was useless; he thought it was a laugh. When we'd finished and I had to take the pony in, he jumped on the cart even though I didn't want him with me, and all the way down to town he was saying, 'Mek it run, mek it run.' My way was to let the pony take its time as it had been working all day. However, as we were going down the Wicker, he grabbed the whip and lashed the pony and, startled, it shot forward into a gallop. I always turned left onto Stanley Street but, under the circumstances, I should have carried straight on under the arches and up Spital Hill. Foolishly, I still tried to turn onto Stanley Street and the next second, I hit the big lamp standard on the corner: the cart had skidded and hit the lamp post, smashing the left-hand side shaft. I told Titch Scott to fuck off, even though I didn't usually swear. I managed to tie the broken shaft together and get the pony and the cart back up to the stable, and when I got home and told my dad what had happened, to say he wasn't pleased is an understatement. I still had to fetch the pony out as usual the next day and get the shaft repaired, but I think he sold that turnout shortly afterwards.

One of the ponies we had was a lovely old mare. We had her for what seems a good few months before my dad sold her to a friend of his, a man called Albert Murphy, who lived at the bottom of Matilda Street, near Shoreham Street, with his wife and young son, Brian. They used to come up to our house quite often, on Sunday afternoons or nights. One Sunday they came up and he was very upset because during that week he'd had an accident near the bus garage at the beginning of Shoreham Street. A bus had hit his pony and cart, knocking down the pony and running over its legs, killing it.

Another time, my dad bought a pony and harness without having a stable for it, so he tied the pony to a clothes pole in our back garden for the night. Fortunately, it stayed put and we stabled it the following day. Then we had an old roan pony. He had bought it off a man who lived on the Arbourthorne estate, behind what is now the KFC takeaway in City Road and where the old stables used to be. It was a Whit Sunday and I was dressed up in my new suit. It was just after dinner time when he said to me, 'Ah've bought a pony. Go to this bloke's 'ouse', he told me where he lived, 'get the pony and tek it t'stable in Well Road be'ind Ponsfords furniture shop. They know all about it,' meaning the stable owner. It was the last thing I expected on Whit Sunday but I did as I was told. I had to walk it up City Road, on Ridgeway Road, Scarsdale and further to Well Road to put the pony away and it was long after teatime when I got back home. But that sort of thing was nothing new. I once had to walk a pony all the way to Masbrough Street in Rotherham because my dad had been down in Castlefolds Wholesale Fruit Market with the pony and cart and, parked on the setts, got talking to a rag man from Rotherham. Next thing, he's sold him the pony, just like that. The bloke only wanted the pony and harness and not the flat cart, so my father left the cart on the setts, and I had to walk the pony to Rotherham. But the last one I remember was a roan pony. It was old and quiet but it would pull its heart out for you.

An old man named Billy Myers, who must have been at least 70 years old, had a small house-windowed fruit shop on Cricket Inn Road. He also did a bit of street hawking around the bottom of Wybourn, and he had a little brown pony, only about three or four years old and very fiery. Myers was scared when he took it out because of it showing off, so my dad did a swap for the old, quiet roan. I think Myers also gave him a few quid. Well, my dad thought he could handle this pony – he was wrong. At this time, we were stabling behind Nunnery Pit, off Manor Lane. The first morning we went down and got the pony harnessed up it started showing off. We got it into the cart to go up the rough-made road to get it onto Manor Lane but it didn't want to know about pulling a cart, so by the time we got to Manor Lane my dad thought it was going to kick the cart to bits and we had to take it back. We kept trying with it all that week but it was unmanageable. Finally my dad declared, 'It's fuckin' mad,' and a couple of days later he said to me, 'Go an' tell Tubby Evans I want to see 'im.' (Tubby was another one who was always at our house. He was about 25 and lived on Boundary Road with his mother.) My dad told him he needed him early the next morning, and so the next day we went to the stable together and got the pony into the yard. This pony was as fat as a pig, and my dad told Tubby, 'It's fuckin' useless an' it's eatin' its fuckin' 'ead off.' He put it into a halter and bridle and making sure they were both strong and firm, got it out onto the track leading to Manor Lane. We also wrapped an old coat around its head so its eyes were covered up, and then we set off up Manor Lane, Tubby Evans and me holding onto its head. At the time, Manor Lane was just that: quite narrow, broken-down stone walls, fields and no houses. We were heading for one of the farms up there that belonged to a man called Harry Cooper. A couple of times on our way up we heard a car coming down and had to get the pony over the wall into the field whilst hanging onto its head as it tried to breakaway, which it nearly did. If it had got loose, we would never have caught it again. We got to the top of Manor lane, into a yard and then into a stable where we left it: my dad had sold it as horse meat because he said that was all it was good for. He sold several horses as meat and never gave it a second thought. Then he bought another horse and also what had been a milk float with rubber tyres which, I think, made it harder for the horse to pull.

A typical tatter – could have been me and my dad

CHAPTER 6

THREE JAM JARS A RIDE

The war was at its height, and there were bombed buildings all over Sheffield. Also in Sheffield were a lot of coal merchants, mostly centred around the wharf and canal area. One of these merchants was Burnett & Hallamshire Ltd. They were buying the old timbers off the bombed sites, taking them to their yard in Harvest Lane and cutting them into logs and selling them to their coal customers, coal being rationed. My dad went to their offices asking them to sell him some of the logs. They eventually agreed and said he could have two loads per week at 2 shillings per bag, so my dad found a huge sack and we were in business. We went twice a week and instead of filling the sack by just throwing the logs in any which way, we stacked them very carefully to get in as many as possible, which was a lot. We then went round the Wybourn estate selling them at 4d a log and they flew out. The customers would open their windows and shout out how many they wanted, and my job was to take the logs to the houses and collect the money. We used to start off at the first house at the beginning of Maltravers Road then up Whites Lane and Manor Oaks Road. We rationed them to just four logs per customer and would have sold every one of them before we got to Southend Place, except the half-dozen we kept for ourselves. This lasted for about twelve months until Burnett & Hallamshire ran out of timbers. So back to tatting and hawking.

I was having more and more time off school and the longest I was off for was thirteen weeks. There used to be what was known as the "school copper" and he'd come to your house if you hadn't been to school. This school copper used to come to our house not because I'd been absent but because he always got a pot of tea, had a warm by the fire and talked to my dad about wirelesses. If my dad had and old wireless radio, he'd sell it to him, usually for 5 shillings, as he always bought them for the valves. So the school copper knew I was off school because I was often in the house whilst this was going on, and I used to have two or three weeks off as a matter of course. Then I would get up one morning and my dad would just say, 'Ah think tha can go t' school today.' I'd have to ask my mother to write me a note making some excuse for my being off school and sometimes she would sometimes not, but I would have to go and I'd always be late. At St. Oswald's, often, when I went back to school my stomach would be churning as I walked into the classroom because I'd had to have time off to work. One teacher in particular used to keep me standing at her desk as if she hadn't seen me, and when I offered her the note, she would look me up and down and say something like 'I suppose you've been with your father on his rag cart.' And having got back to school and just about caught up with the lessons, I would be getting ready for school on a morning when my father or mother would suddenly say, 'Tha can give me 'and today.'

There was only one teacher who really had time for me, Miss Crossley, and one day she said to me, 'Derek Naylor, you could be the future Lord Mayor of Sheffield.' More than once when I hadn't gone to school, there was a knock at the back door and my mother would answer it to find a classmate there: 'Miss Crossley says, is your Derek comin' t' school?' and my mother would make some excuse, one of them being, 'Tell 'er 'e's got no shoes.' On this occasion, half an hour later there was another knock and the same classmate's stood there with a pair of old running slippers in his hand, saying, 'Miss Crossley says will these fit your Derek?' It made no difference, I didn't go. And on a Friday afternoon the teacher would remind us that she wanted to see us at Mass on Sunday morning. On one occasion my dad had bought a load of plums to sell. When I told him the teacher had said I had to be at Mass, he said, 'Tell thi teacher to fuck off. Ah'll not 'ave my fuckin' plums goin' rotten.'

As kids, me and our Tets didn't know what it was to go to a barber's as my dad had a pair of shears and a pair of scissors and would cut our hair himself. It would be a short back and sides and took him ages. (I think he fancied himself as a barber.) Other times my mother would have a go, which was even worse. For some reason she would get us when we went home at dinner time (we lived across the road from the school). I'd protest and she'd say, 'I just want t' tek it out thi eyes,' and then she'd start at the back. She could never get it even so she'd take off a bit more and then a bit more until she finally got mad with herself and went completely over the top with the shears. We'd finish up with it all off except for a little tuft in the front, which she used for getting hold of to pull us into the house. Most of the other lads had similar hair cuts, though a lot of them had patches of blue dye all over their heads because they had scabies (and the dye was used to spot them). Of course, nobody was ever bothered about it.

We never had braces and used an old tie or coat belt to hold our trousers up. But every Christmas we'd get new jerseys which we wore all the time until they had big holes at the front, and I mean big,

big holes. When the jerseys were past it, we would cut the sleeves off, sew the ends up and use them as socks and when we got a hole in the heel, we'd turn them upside down. Then we'd turn them round and have a hole either side. Then they were finally thrown away but we certainly got our money's worth out of them! (I once bought myself a pair of socks from the market but when I put them on, I found out they were pit socks – the feet were miles too big and they came up to my thighs. I still wore them.)

I was still getting good hidings, sometimes from him, sometimes my mother. One day she had got me pinned into a corner, hitting me. My father thought she wasn't hitting me hard enough and started in on me as well, using his fist and feet. I'll never forget what my mother shouted at him, 'Don't 'it 'im ont' 'ead, tha'll mek 'im fuckin' daft!' Now, many years later when I think about it, I have a little smile to myself and wonder if she said it too late.

Occasionally I would be able to slip out and have a game of football or marbles, but he didn't like me to be out in case he wanted me to do something or other. One day I was out on Boundary road, about 200 yards away, playing football with the lads that lived on there when I heard him shouting me at the top of his voice. I ignored him. Ten minutes later he was shouting me again but this time he didn't stop, and finally one of the other kids said, 'Na then Derek, thi father's shoutin' thi.' This time I knew I couldn't ignore him, so I started to walk back, and when I got towards the bottom of the path I started to run. Out of breath, as if I had run all the way, I got to the back door, where he was stood on the step. When I asked him what he wanted me for he said, 'Get some fuckin' coil (coal) ont' fire.'

I've spoken about when my mother would borrow money from

Mrs Boardman in the middle of the week. When things were really tight, my mother also used to send me to borrow from her eldest sister, Hilda. Hilda was married to a miner named Herbert and they lived in Brough Street, which was near a big firm called Daniel Doncaster Ltd. on Penistone Road. The first time my mother sent me to Hilda's with a note asking if she could lend her anything, perhaps 4 shillings, until the end of the week, she also gave me 2d for my bus and tram fares (at that time was only a halfpenny bus fare from Southend Place to Pond Street, though later it went up to 1d) and instructions on how to get to Brough Street: Get off the bus at Pond Street. Behind the GPO, go up the stone steps to Fitzalan Square. Go to the last tram stop, near the top of Commercial Street, and get on a tram that says Wadsley Bridge via Woodseats. Get off at the bottom of Bamforth Street. From there it was just a short walk to Aunt Hilda's. So I gave my aunt the note and she grumbled (as she always did) but didn't let me leave empty-handed. I left her house and went to catch a tram back to Fitzalan Square and then realized she hadn't told me how to get back to town – the trams there and back had different destinations on the front and I didn't know which one to get on. I finally decided I'd walk and just follow the tram lines back to town but was puzzled when I got to Hillfoot Bridge because one set went straight on whilst another turned left. I decided to follow the ones that went straight on and, eventually, got back to near the market, by which time I knew where I was. After that, I went a few times to Hilda's. She had a daughter and also two sons who I got on well with, though both were a bit older than me, and the younger one, Ron, used to come up to our house on a Sunday because there was always something going on. Seventy years on I still see him, and we are still good friends.

I think it was around 1943, when I would have been 10 years old, we started making toys to sell. We were working in the kitchen, and set up on the table were a circular saw, a vice and other tools. They were arguing back and forth, again. My mother had been poking the fire up with a big bastard file when, shouting something at her, he started to shove the door open to say something else. As he started to open the door, she turned round, file still in her hand and threw it at him. His reaction was so fast he pulled the door back shut, good job. He went as white as a sheet and so did she because she had thrown it just as if it were a throwing knife and it hit the door and the tang stuck in the door, just where his neck would have been. When they pulled the tang out, a huge splinter of wood came with it. The door was like that for years, as a reminder.

We carried on making toys, with the kitchen as a proper workshop. (The circular saw was plugged into the electric light.) We made tanks, lorries, dolls, dolls' cots, scooters (all painted green), and he was taking orders left, right and centre, mostly in pubs. I would go to Turner's hardware stall in the rag market to buy little wooden wheels and Mudfords on Sheaf Street for bundles of wood. After a while my dad went round one or two shops looking for orders, and he got a good one from a newsagent shop on Langsett Road. We still had the horse and cart, and he was going out tatting during the day, so we had to make the toys at night. We then got an order from a bloke called Jimmy McTigue, who lived in Boundary Road, to make him some little bats with a hole in the centre. He was making bats and balls (the ball being on a piece of elastic) and selling them in Skegness. We had a job getting hold of the plywood but, anyhow, we made up this order for the shop in Langsett Road, got them on the cart and delivered them to the shop. When we got there, my dad went into the shop and thirty seconds later he's back out. The owner had told him to get lost. He didn't want them because it was only two or three days before Christmas and my dad had never thought that the shop owner wanted them in time to be able to sell them by Christmas. So going back to town, we were racking our brains about what to do with them when, finally, my dad said, 'Ah know what,' and we went down and stood just outside the bottom entrance to the rag and tag market. Within about two hours we'd sold the lot, thank God, but I never used to get paid anything.

The following year he came across a bloke in Doncaster market selling small stiff paper hats in paper bags. The hats had little stickers on the front saying KISS ME QUICK or HOLD ME TIGHT and the like. My dad thought this would be worth copying so he found somewhere to buy the hats, while my mother made him a dyed red-ish coloured cloak out of an old army blanket, and a cotton wool beard. The hats were put in bags so you didn't know which one said what, and Father Christmas sold "lucky dip" bags at 6d a dip at the bottom of Dixon Lane.

I'd been spending a reasonable amount of time at school, and it was time for me to take the 11 plus (as it was called then) and with it the possibility of passing the scholarship. The whole class sat the exam and some weeks later when the results were announced, it turned out that quite a few had passed, including me. It was explained to us that if we wanted to go to a grammar school (Notre Dame or De La Salle), we'd have to attend school for an extra year. So I got up early, got ready for school and waited for my dad to come downstairs. I then waited until he'd got himself a pot of tea before telling him about passing the exam and that I would have to go to school for an additional year. I remember very clearly what he said: 'No. We've kept tha all these years, na tha can fuckin' keep us for a change.' It was never spoken of again; my mother never ever said a word about it.

My dad got another pony and also bought what was called a "tub", a cart that you could ride in with a little door at the back, big wheels and little mud guards. It was the summer time, and so on Saturdays we started giving kids rides at dinner time. We could get four or five kids in the cart but as the kids didn't have any money, we charged them three jam jars a ride. Within minutes there would be a queue of kids at the bottom of our path, all with three jam jars in their hands. My dad would take the jars off them and lift them into the cart, and then I would turn the pony around, go down the street and onto Boundary Road, then turn around and come back. About half way back I'd give the pony a little flick of the reins for a trot. By now, my dad would have bagged-up the jars on the back door-step, and when he lifted the kids off the cart, they'd dash off to find another three jars each. This could go on all afternoon, sometimes until six or seven o'clock, and so there would be sacks and sacks of jars outside our back door. Monday morning he would take them down to where we weighed in the rags, and the price he got was one shilling per dozen for the 1 lb jars and 1/6 for the 2 lb ones. I used to think there wouldn't be a single jar left on the estate.

There was a cowboy film on at the Park cinema, which was at the bottom of South Street, and I really wanted to see this picture but I needed 7d to get in plus 2d bus fare. I thought that if I worked hard all day and asked my dad for the money he would give it to me. I'd never asked him for anything before. Whenever I had a few coppers, I would have earned them by running errands, selling sticks (firewood) and so forth. And there was an old lady, Mrs Pitts, who lived opposite us in Southend Place who had taken a liking to me and wouldn't have anyone else do things for her. She always paid me with a brass threepenny bit and would often shout me to her front door and give me a pair of shoes. These would be worn but in good condition and well polished and fitted me, and over the years I had many pairs of shoes from her. I understand she worked at a big house, in service, and would have got the shoes from her employer – but back to the jam jars. I worked non-stop all day with the rides. The picture started at 6 o'clock but it was continuous, so you could go in up to 7 o'clock and still see the whole picture, except you saw the end of the film before you saw the beginning of it but that didn't matter. I started asking my dad for the picture money about 3 o'clock and although he said no, I thought that eventually I would get it and kept asking, about every half hour. He kept saying no and late on he got nasty, and by the time it was six o'clock or just after, I realized I wasn't going to the pictures, despite my working hard. (And I've just realized he would have had to stable the pony himself.) I never asked him or my mother for anything again.

Just before the war ended, my dad rented a little workshop on West Street in what is now Morton Works and started mirror polishing. The workshop only had one spindle and he was getting a bit of work from a small cutlery manufacturer called Flemming & Co. on Bath Street, and then for Rawson Bros. Ltd, and Thomas Turton Ltd, both, I think, in Rockingham Street. The main man at

Turton's was Alderman Bywaters, ex Sheffield councillor and Lord Mayor. He was very good to my father and when my father saw a car for sale in Gilder's showroom, at the top of Cambridge Street, he went with my dad to look it over and give his opinion. The car was a 1936 Morris Eight and, I think, about £80. He then paid for the car and let my dad pay it back at £2 per week out of the money he had to come at the end of each week.

My mother was going down to help him with the work and she would get home at about 5.30 p.m. and sometimes say, 'Thi dad's workin' o'er whilst ah get tea ready.' By about 7.30 when he hadn't come home, she would start getting mad and say, 'Ah bet 'e's gone int' Saddle!' (This pub was next door to the workshop and is still there.) And she'd give me 2d bus fare and say, 'Get down there an' find 'im an' get 'im 'ome!' So off I would go and finding the workshop locked up, I'd just open the door to The Saddle and look in. Sometimes he was sat with a man called Jim, who came from Manchester and, it turned out, was a deserter from Shirecliffe Army Barracks. (My dad eventually brought him home to stay at our house for a few weeks.) But there he'd be, sat in his mucky clothes, and when I told him my mam was mad, his reply would be, 'Ah've only jus' come in.' Well, I'd get my dad onto the tram, half drunk, but he would never sit down, and since he wasn't tall enough to hold on to the leather strap above him, he'd be staggering about and wanting to talk to everyone. Then I'd get him to Pond Street and on the bus until it got to the Windsor Hotel and he'd want to go in. I sometimes had to literally push him down Boundary Road, and then we'd go over the Dunn's garden (our neighbours) and to our back door where my mother would be wailing on the step, and then she'd give him hell. If Jim was there (also drunk), he would tell my mother to leave my dad alone and she'd tell him to mind 'is own fuckin' business. Eventually things got a bit hot for him as a deserter, and he had to go on the run again.

My dad moved into a bigger workshop in Leah's Yard (now a listed building) on Cambridge Street. I remember it well because so much of it was original. In the yard there was a massive steam engine which drove all the machinery in practically every workshop. Everything was belt driven via shafting throughout the building, and lighting was by gas mantles on walls. The washing facility was just a bucket of water heated up by the steam from a pipe in the yard. There was no such thing as a dust extraction system, and it was very mucky work. This was where I learned about mirror polishing. I used to strip the glazers and dress them up ready for the next day. (A glazer is a small, hard felt disc screwed onto a spindle end and painted with glue or cement before being rolled in emery powder and used as an abrasive in polishing.) But my dad wouldn't move with the times by doing such things as investing in electric spindles; he stayed with the old belt-driven type with shafting and the gas mantle lighting. Gradually, work dried up and he had got fed up with mirror polishing, so it was back to hawking, chimney sweeping and whatever else.

The type of tub we used for the jam jar rides

CHAPTER 7

CHOCOLATE TOFFEE APPLES

Throughout the war years things got tighter and tighter and everything was rationed, including coal. My brother and I started going down Manor Lane and behind the Nunnery Pit to where they tipped the slag and waste from the pit. In this waste there would be little pieces of coal which we would pick out and put into a sack. We went down to this tip straight after school for about an hour, and then with a sack on our shoulder we'd get off home. We worked independently of each other, and my brother always used to be home before me. This tip was a well-known place for picking coal and at times there would be as many as ten to fifteen men, women and kids picking, all with prams, barrows and bikes to carry it home. We'd all wait for the tubs to come up from the pit bottom and there'd be a mad scramble when they were tipped but we always managed to get something, and we always had a fire. As I've already mentioned, there was a big family in Southend Road called the Gurnhills. Mr Gurnhill had a huge barrow – it was five to six feet long. One Sunday it was decided that instead of just going on the tip, we would go onto the railway siding in Woodbourne Road where there would be railway wagons filled with coal from Nunnery Colliery. So on this Sunday morning, me; my brother; Mr Gurnhill; his brother-in-law (who was a bit slow on the uptake) and Mr Gurnhill's two eldest sons, Edward and Roy, all went off to the railway siding. There was never much traffic about and everything was quiet. The train lines ran under a bridge on Woodbourne Road, so we had to go down a bank before we could climb up onto the wagons and then throw the biggest lumps of coal off the wagon whilst the others carried it up the bank and threw it into the barrow. All this time my heart was racing. I had done many things but nothing as risky as this. Eventually the barrow was filled (there must have been a good 5-6 cwt in it) and we all pushed and pulled it up Manor Lane onto Maltravers Terrace and back to Gurnhill's house. There, we got about 2 cwt of it and the Gurnhills had the rest, but we never went back to the siding a second time.

One of the last episodes involving a horse and cart was when my dad bought a pony and harness from a man who had been coming round selling ice cream. The ice-cream cart was horse drawn, and as the summer was nearly over, my dad bought the horse and cart from him. Because we already had a cart, we only used the ice-cream one when we were selling logs. So, we were out tatting again. (I was 10 or 11 years old and off school, again.) One week, a pal of my dad's called Tommy Goodwin had come up to our house and he ended up stopping for some time and coming out tatting with us. He never really did anything, just walked beside the cart or on the pavement, but he was getting his grub and somewhere to sleep, and I know my dad always gave him something out of what we weighed in for, while I never got anything. They were cold, rainy, miserable days and we'd go out and have hardly anything to show for it, but on this particular morning it was obvious my dad had flu, and he said he couldn't go out so we'd have to go without him. Minutes later, Tommy Goodwin said, 'Ah think ah'm goin' to get off, Lol. Ah 'aven't seen us kids this week an' ah'm wonderin' if they're alright.'

And off he went. But Tommy was useless anyway; he suffered with TB and would never have work.

I preferred to go out on my own. I could handle the pony, and shouting in the street didn't bother me, I was used to it. I got ready, went and got the pony out and went down to the market, parking the pony on the setts. Having 4 or 5 shillings of my own in my pocket, I went into Woolworth's and bought half a dozen tea plates and a couple of small basins before setting off tatting. I worked the Arbourthorne, Manor, and Woodthorpe estates, staying out until around 4 o'clock, and then I went to Elliotts to weigh-in; I drew £2 and 4s and was really proud of myself. After that I went to Messrs Frost & Co., the corn merchants on Sheaf Street, to get feed for the pony, went to the stable to feed and water it and put it away for the night and then went home. When I got in, I told him how I'd gone on for the day and gave him the money I'd made. I don't think I got so much as a thank you or well done. On another occasion, we had been out tatting around the Martin Street area when my dad stopped at the bottom of Scotland Street where there was a cobbler's and clog maker's shop, and he went in while I looked after the cart. On the cart was a brass coal scuttle and a woman going past spotted it and asked how much I wanted for it. Not knowing how much to ask I said half-a-crown. She gave me the money and was off like a shot. When my dad came out he missed the scuttle straight away, and when I told him how much I'd sold it for, he called me every name he could think of. By this time the good hidings had just about stopped, though years later when I was talking with my younger brother, Lawrence, about it and asked him if he used to get the pastings I got, he said he had done a few times. Then, finally, as my dad went to hit him, he said, "it me just once more an' ah'll fuckin' kill tha!' And my dad never hit him again. I was amazed to hear this, that he had threatened his father! When I told him I could never think of hitting my dad, even when I was big enough and strong enough, he said I was daft.

For our next venture, when I was 12 or 13 years old, we started making toffee apples which we sold from the house for 3d or 4d each. My dad also got the idea to become a painter and decorator. He bought a spray gun, which worked off a vacuum cleaner, from Wilks hardware shop on Norfolk Street and a device used for creating a wood grain effect on doors, etc. and then practiced on everything he could think of. He got his first job painting the kitchen and staircase for a friend who lived in Thornborough Road, Arbourthorne. He was Bill Lee and he and his wife had, I think, six kids. He'd been a pal of my dad's for years and had started a business making small tools in Sudbury Street, off Meadow Street. We set-to on the kitchen but my dad wouldn't use a brush; he used the spray gun on everything. The kitchen was painted green and cream and then given a coat of varnish. He did round the fireplace and then we started on the staircase. We were at it most of the week and I remember the Friday teatime because Bill's wife cooked a hot tea and put some out for us, as well. So I stood round the table with her kids eating mashed potatoes, sprouts, bacon (and the bacon fat over the potatoes) and bread and butter and tea. It was a real feast, fit for a king, and I quickly cleared my plate. However, there were affects from the decorating because the varnish took so long to dry, and Mrs Lee complained that everything they touched was sticky for weeks after. That was the end of the decorating business.

So then my dad had another brainwave: he bought a roll of roofing felt, and we already had a lot of part-full tins of paint in the pantry. He cut lengths off the roll and sprayed them different colours with the paint sprayer so that the colours mingled together before drying. The idea was to put the pieces down as floor covering in front of the sink. Again, the idea was fine, it just didn't work because whilst he'd taken orders for them, customers were coming back saying their feet were sticking to the paint. So we went back to the toffee apples.

For a change, this one was a winner and we were really selling a lot of them; in fact, the toffee apples were keeping us! In addition to selling them from the house, my dad got an old apple box, covered it with the roofing felt, painted it sky blue and put a strap on it using a piece of a horse harness so that it was like the trays used in cinemas for selling ice creams. We were in business! My mother was getting Ostermilk baby food and Colact, a baby milk food flavoured with chocolate powder, and we had the idea of dipping the toffee apples in the Colact to stop them sticking to the paper bags we put them in, so we called them chocolate toffee apples. We went round Castlefolds Market where my dad would buy 20-30 boxes of eating apples at a time, 40lb in each one, and we'd stack them up at the bottom of the stairs. I had to dash home from school at four o'clock to help make the chocolate toffee apples as it had become a family enterprise – my mam, dad, me and my brother all working at it. When they were ready, I would wash my hands and face while my dad got his white smock on, then I'd put the leather strap over my head and, carrying the box in front of me just like they did at the pictures, we would set off down Maltravers Terrace. I'd walk down the middle of the road, my dad near the pavement, both of us shouting, 'Chocolate toffee apples 3d and 4d! Chocolate toffee apples!' The box held 120 apples, and I'd serve while my dad took the money. We'd go out six nights a week at about five o'clock and on Sunday afternoons. But come the bank holiday he did his usual trick of getting blind drunk and, still drunk, getting up in the night for a pee. Having got to the bottom of the stairs and thinking he was in the toilet, he pissed all over the boxes of apples. When my mother got up the next morning it was like a flood, and she went mad at him, calling him every name under the sun as she cleaned it up. We still used the apples but he didn't even wash them, just left them to dry.

In 1945 my dad decided that the horse and cart was a thing of the past because a horse had to be fed seven days a week and you could get around faster in a motor vehicle. So one Sunday morning I went with him to buy a little Ford pick-up truck, which I think he paid about £40 for, from someone on the Parson Cross estate. Though we started hawking with it, he didn't have a proper driving licence, only a provisional one, but this was a minor consideration; I think at the time regulations had been relaxed because of the war. We started going out to a potato merchant called Lomas, at Dinnington, who are still in business and supply chip shops. We were buying what were known as "pig potatoes". They were good potatoes but because they were meant only for feeding pigs, there was a blue powder sprinkled in the top of every sackfull; however, if you took out the ones covered in powder, you were left with plenty of good potatoes. So we'd go out hawking using these potatoes as a loss leader at 10lb for a shilling and this was a big draw so we did reasonably well. One area we did was the Parkwood Springs estate, where Sheffield Ski Village now is, but the estate was a little world of its own, built over very steep hills and with just one road in. We also supplied a couple of cafes there, at 10/- a bag, and a small pub at the top of the estate. The publican was called Bill Riley, a big, imposing figure of a man who also worked as a commissionaire at Batchelor Foods in Claywheels Lane, and as my dad knew him from when they were kids, he always had a pint with him when we were up there. Also at the top lived a woman named Edna Houseley, a widow with four kids, the youngest being only a few months old. We'd call on her because we always got a pot of tea. She was often breast feeding the baby and this always fascinated me. The baby would be suckling on what looked just like a little flat hot-water bottle, but she wasn't at all embarrassed by our being there (or by my presence) and just carried on whilst talking to my dad. It turned out she was an old flame of my dad's and when my mother knew we'd been up to Parkwood Springs, she would say to me, 'Ah suppose 'e 'ad to call at Edna 'ouseley's?' and she would get mad at him.

Thinking it would be a good idea to turn the old Ford pick-up (a 1930s model) into a van, my dad bought an old van body from a scrapyard up Grenoside. When we got back to Southend Place, we took the pick-up body off and fastened battens to the chassis to extend it then put on the van body. We had to keep reversing it into the house wall to shove it on and now that it was three or four feet longer (and bigger all round) it looked very odd. After converting the pick-up, he started taking fishing trips. He was never short of petrol coupons and could get eight or ten blokes in the van, sitting on their baskets. On his last trip in this van, he was coming down Handsworth Hill when he ran into the back of a car on account of his brakes not being very good. He was able to get the men out before the police arrived, but they had to walk the rest of the way home. He then swapped the van for a big ex-army Dodge Shooting Brake so he could continue with the fishing trips at weekends, but he wasn't making any money out of it and the Dodge was a real petrol grabber, and as he was buying black market petrol at double the price, that idea went out the window. It was back to a horse and cart.

We'd been going up Rivelin during the six weeks' school holiday and round the estates on Sundays selling the toffee apples. I fact, we were doing so well my dad was buying apples forty boxes at a time, and when apples were short we used pears, and when there were no apples or pears to be had we went on to toffee popcorn. Sweets were still on ration (almost everything was on ration), so me and my brother had to go round town with all our ration books buying golden syrup and puffed wheat. My mother boiled the syrup with a bit of butter and a dash of vinegar until it turned into toffee, then quickly poured it into a huge bowl of puffed wheat whilst stirring it all together. When ready it was put into 2oz bags (making 120 bags!) then into the sky-blue apple box and off round the estate selling toffee popcorn at 3d a bag. Some years later, on my first date with my future wife, we were walking down Maltravers Terrace and the kids started shouting after us, 'Threepence a bag, threepence a bag' at the top of their voices. I just grinned to myself.

The war over, all the soldiers were being demobbed but came back to find there were no jobs to be had, so a lot of them started their own small businesses. One of these was a Mr Marsden, whose wife and two daughters lived in Southend Place. He was a painter and decorator. One day he came across to our house at teatime and said that he'd just got a job to do in City Road and would one of us lads be interested in moving his ladders, which were on a barrow, from the job that he'd just finished to this job in City Road. When he said he'd pay 4 shillings, me and my brother Terrence both jumped at the chance, but then my dad said I was going out with him so my brother got the job and after that he got to move his ladders a few times.

During the earlier times when we had a horse and cart and were going out hawking, Fridays and Saturdays were the two main days. We would go round the Castlefolds Wholesale Market to buy all we needed, starting off with five bags of potatoes, 1cwt in each bag. By the time we'd loaded up everything, the cart was piled high and always overweight, but my dad never gave a thought to how the pony was going to pull it up all the hills onto the Wybourn. We'd set off up Broad Street, past the Durham Ox pub and up Whites Lane, he at the pony's head, me behind the cart pushing as hard as I could up the hills to help the pony. At times I used to feel so bitter towards him but I just had to get on with it, though on one occasion we had just got to the start of Maltravers Road and he was using the whip on the pony when a woman going past saw what he was doing and, turning back, gave him a real tongue lashing. I think she would have taken the whip off him and used it on him if she could have.

During the war years, there had been a bloke called Ned also hawking round the top of the Wybourn. He lived with his sister and brother-in-law, who had a fish and chip shop at the bottom of Manor Lane, near St. Aidan's Church. Ned only sold potatoes and greens, and while he was only thin, he was as strong as an ox and used to pull a handcart up Manor Lane, shouting at the top of his voice. (He was also a bit eccentric.) My dad thought that no-one else should hawk round the Wybourn, only him. So when we were out Fridays and Saturdays, we tried to get round the streets before him. Then a man called Jimmy Ogden, who had just left the army and was living on Manor Oaks Road, started hawking on the Wybourn again. My dad didn't like this competition, and what's more, Terrence started working Saturdays for Jimmy and would be up and out before my dad could stop him. This all ended when Jimmy's horse, which he used to tether on some wasteland behind his house, strangled itself one night. After a while Jimmy got a handcart, so my brother went back to working Saturdays, helping to push the cart. My brother wasn't afraid of hard work, he just didn't like working for nothing. He had more sense than me.

My sister Brenda and brothers Terrence and Lawrence
– Whit Sunday, late 1940s

CHAPTER 8

"STOP ME AND BUY ONE"

I was now 12 or 13 and growing up. During early summer there would be a glut of cauliflowers so they were really cheap, and we'd get a cart load from the market and go round the streets selling them at 8d each or two for a shilling. We did the areas where a lot of the houses shared yards and we usually sold all the cauliflowers we had. We were doing more and more hawking and now bananas were coming onto the scene and though my dad had to pay over the odds for them, they brought in the customers, who got two or three bananas if they bought our vegetables.

The next thing was sweeping chimneys and occasionally someone would want a piece of furniture moving, sometimes a piano, for which my dad would charge £2. (Someone told me of the time they were moving a piano in Wentworth Street and it had to come down a steep entry. My dad was at the front trying to hold it back but he couldn't and it ran away with him. I'd like to have seen that.) My dad would try anything and everything and I remember him saying that when he was a teenager, he came up with the idea of going out with a little tin of paint and a brush and painting people's letterboxes and house numbers for 2d a time. And on one occasion he bought some tulips which were drooping, as tulips do, and the petals were falling off so he tried sticking them back on with condensed milk before selling them!

In 1948, when I was 15, it was time for me to leave school. I clearly remember my last day. It was August and school, as usual, was breaking up for the six weeks' holiday. So at 3 o'clock on this Friday afternoon it was assembly in the hall for prayers and a rounding-off of the term and, finally, home time. Just like any other home time. (There was no careers officer to help you find a job and no-one asked what you wanted to do or be.) When I got home, it was set the cart out and then, by 5 o'clock, off down the street and onto Hazelhurst Road. We might have gone a hundred yards and I hadn't opened my mouth to shout, so my dad turned round to me and said, 'What's up with tha? Can't tha fuckin' shout?' I'd left school alright.

By this time my mother had had two more sons. (At 12 years old I had to baby-sit Lawrence when he was born in 1945.) It was the week after I left school that my mother, having been in confinement, gave birth to another little boy, Graham, on the Saturday morning. I took her a cup of tea, and she asked me if my dad had given me any money. I said yes and she asked how much. When I told her £2 10s, she said, 'Right, give me two pound and keep ten shillin' for yoursen.' That was that and I carried on working for my dad.

Graham only lived for fourteen months. I don't know why but right from day one I loved my little brother. I looked after him – making up his bottle and feeding him, winding him, getting him off to sleep – and I never got tired of getting down on the floor and playing with him. But he fell ill and was rushed into Lodge Moor Hospital. A few days later I was setting the cart out when a woman came up the street, up our path and knocked on the front door. My father came to the door and she said to him, 'Mr Naylor, 'ave you got a little boy in Lodge Moor 'ospital?' He said yes and then she said, 'Mr Naylor, we 'ave just 'ad a phone call askin' us to tell tha that thi little boy 'as just died.' She was a cleaner at The Windsor Hotel in Boundry Road. After she had gone, I just sat on the front step; I had never felt such pain and sadness as I did at that moment and while I have done since, I will always remember that morning.

In 1950, twelve months after Graham died, my mother had another baby, a little girl she named Gloria. Shortly after Gloria's birth, I took my mother up a cup of tea in bed. It was wrong of me, I know that now, but I resented her having this little girl because I thought it hadn't taken my mother long to get over Graham and, at first, I wouldn't look at the baby. My mother must have realized how I felt because as I was leaving the bedroom, she called me back and asked me to look at baby Gloria. I did so, reluctantly. But now I realize how wrong I was, that she had had Gloria to try to ease her pain at losing Graham.

Six months after leaving school, I was taken on at Millsands Rolling Mills, where there were about a dozen lads, all dogsbodies. There was a certain amount of jostling and I finished up having two fights in quick succession. The first lad was a pushover but the other was vicious. We went out onto some waste ground – this wasn't a pushing and wrestling fight, it was toe to toe, and fists, and lasted about twenty minutes. We had quite a crowd around us, and the women were shouting for someone to stop the fight. It ended when we were both exhausted. Neither of us won but neither lost, and afterwards the lads and boys who worked there showed us a lot of respect. But I didn't like working there and went back to hawking.

Not long after leaving Millsands, we were coming down Wallace Road from Parkwood Springs when my dad pulled up outside Hallamshire Rolling Mills and went inside. A few minutes later he came out and said, 'Come wi' me, ah've got thee a job.' A bloke looked at my dad, looked at me, said, "ow old are tha?' and when I told him 15, he said, 'Right, start Monday mornin', six o'clock.' My wage was just over £4 a week. Well, I hated it. Mornings and afternoons I was hooking-up in the wire mill. I only weighed about eight and a half stone, and when I got the hook under a red-hot billet, my feet left the floor because I wasn't heavy enough and the roller would be shouting at me, 'For fucks sake, get thissen under it!' as he tried to shove it back through the rolls. One afternoon, one of the men asked me if my dad ever bought bits of non-ferrous scrap. I said yes and he told me that he had a bit of lead in his cellar, so I mentioned it to my dad and we went to this bloke's house where he fetched it up. Though he was a big, strong bloke, he struggled with it. Testing how much it weighed, my dad managed to lift it off the floor but by only about two inches, just. He said, 'Ah think there's about 4 stone 'ere,' and made him an offer, which he accepted, though there must have been at least a hundredweight there. We took it to Kelvin Metals in Landsett Road to weigh it in and, as usual, I didn't get a penny off him … and I never used to ask.

After my birthday the foreman came to me and said, 'Are tha 16 now?' and when I said yes, he told me, 'Right, tha's on nights next week.' I did two weeks and that was enough. I think my mother knew that I didn't like it and when I gave her my wages that week (I tipped all up), what was left for my spending money covered my bus fares with just a little bit left over. She looked at me and said, 'Ah don't know 'ow ah'd manage wi'out your money cos thi father's not doin' much.' I'm sure this was pressure on me not to pack in the job; however, my dad went and got a job mirror polishing at A. H. Bisby

Ltd, Murray Works, Portobello Place, near Jessops Hospital, and within a week of him starting there, he was saying how good a job it was and wanting me to join him, which I did. I had a good idea of how to do the job and we worked together doing piecework.

Mr Bisby was a self-made man. It was said that he was brought up in a home, perhaps Fulwood Cottage Homes or Barnardo's. When elderly he was a bit like Winston Churchill – stocky build and gruff voice. It was also said that he'd got on his feet through a series of factory fires. Cutlery knife handles were made of Xylonite, which was highly flammable and burned fiercely when ignited, and it was common for cutlery firms to catch fire. Apparently, Bisby's had a number of them but when the last one happened, he was refused insurance until he had a sprinkler system installed right through the factory, which was a big one. Bisby was employing over 200 people at the time and every morning he would walk through the factory and speak to everyone, even a 16 year old. (I remember that an old man my dad knew, a Mr Gillott, had a small cutlery workshop on Leah's Yard. He also had a series of fires but when he had the last one, he was too embarrassed to go to the insurance company to collect the cheque, so he paid my Uncle George to go instead.)

There was an institution like an approved school at the top of Shirecliffe Lane where many teenaged boys were sent by the courts. Bisby employed a number of these boys, mostly in the forge, helping them to get on their feet, and it was commonly believed that he did this because he had been brought up in a boys' home himself. One day he sent for my dad and asked him if he would consider taking one of the boys (who worked in the forge) into our home. The lad in question, tall and pasty-faced, aged about 17, had almost finished

72

his sentence and would have to move out of the institution. His name was Gordon McNulty and though he came from somewhere near Coventry, he wanted to stay in Sheffield but had nowhere to go. My dad talked to my mother about it and she said yes, but as we lived in a two-bedroomed council house, he had to sleep with me and my brother in the back bedroom. He gave my mother a weekly board, and she got him kitted out with underclothes, shoes, a suit for the weekends, the lot. After a while, he started going to see his family at weekends, with the encouragement of my mother, and eventually, after being with us for ten or eleven months, he went to back home to live with them.

By now my brother Terrence had also left school and he joined us at Bisby's a few months later. However, my dad soon started taking advantage. He'd say he wasn't feeling very well and for us two to get off and that he'd be down later, yet he still expected to take the lion's share of whatever we earned. Well, my brother soon decided he'd put a stop to this by telling the wages clerk how much to put in the wage packet for my dad but it made no difference and he still got what he wanted. My brother left the firm after six to eight months and whilst I decided to go self-employed, I still worked side by side with my dad.

One afternoon a young girl who worked in the office came to my dad and said someone wanted to see him in the yard. About ten or fifteen minutes later he came back and was very subdued. When I asked what was wrong, he said his eldest brother, George, had come to tell him that his father had just died. I had seen my grandfather quite often as my dad used to take me up to see him every Whit Sunday and they'd go to the pub, and we often called in to see him when we were out hawking. He always seemed a rather stern man and appeared to disapprove of my dad not having a proper job. When his wife (my dad's mother) died in 1934, he went to live with a lady called Mrs Cunningham. I'm sure she looked after him well but everything was very prim and proper. (He worked as a road sweeper in later life and I'm sure he would have been the best road sweeper in the county.) But in all the times I saw him, he never once spoke to me or asked how I was doing at school, or why I wasn't at school. I believe he was 68 when he died, and my uncles insisted that I, as the eldest grandson, should be the first to follow behind his coffin, alone, so this I did. He was buried in City Road Cemetery, and by the time I took my leave through the cemetery gates, I had forgotten all about him. Which is sad but a fact.

I was very happy at Bisby's and stayed there until I was called up the age of 18. It was mucky work but that didn't bother me; besides, I was my own boss and earning £7 a week. My mother had £4 10s board and I paid my own expenses (such as bus fares) from the rest. At Christmas Mr Bisby used to arrange a proper Christmas dinner, and everyone got a Christmas box. My first year I received £2 and I went straight down to Cann's music shop, top of Dixon Lane, and bought myself a mouth organ. (I got pretty good at it.)

During this time, we still had a go at different ventures and on Saturday mornings I'd go out with an original Wall's "Stop Me and Buy One" bike, selling ice cream. My dad bought a 1931 James three-wheeler van which had been turned into an ice-cream van. It had cast iron wheels and a two cylinder J.A.P. air-cooled engine, with the starting handle in the side of the body. It was very powerful (you could have pulled a tank with it) and had a very short clutch, about three inches, so if you let it out fast, the front wheel would jump about a foot off the ground. This van was very primitive but my dad loved it. (About seventy years later, there was a photo of its "twin" in the Sheffield Metro and from what was said about its history, I felt it could have been the same one!)

We were buying our ice cream from an Italian ice-cream maker called Caira, whose factory was in Pitt Street, just off West Street. My dad would go back home in the van whilst I had to peddle and push the "Stop Me" bike up Granville Road, City Road and Manor Lane. Then we'd sort out the ice cream and lollipops and set off. I only went out selling on Saturdays and Sundays but if it was a nice day, my dad would take the day off work and go out selling ice cream. And sometimes on a Friday he would even be selling it outside Bisby's. I worked the Wybourn and Manor Park and whilst I stayed up top for as long as I could, eventually I'd have to go downhill, knowing that I'd have to push it all back uphill again. But one thing, I

was very fit! After the first year, I bought a motorized ice-cream bike off Caira. It was just like a "Stop Me and Buy One" but with a motorbike engine. It was known as a Dot, and it was a real flash, quite ornately sign-painted in cream and gold. I paid £45 for it.

My mother and Lawrence (1946-7)

CHAPTER 9

JAM TOMORROW

When I was called up for National Service in 1951, I joined the RAF, signing up for four years. The pay was better than I'd previously earned, so I put the Dot in a yard at the bottom of Duke Street for the winter. (When I went for it at the start of the following summer, it had gone. My dad had sold it.) Getting my papers and reporting to the RAF recruiting office in Cambridge Street, I found there were about a dozen of us. We went down to Victoria Station and then on to a place called Cardington, in Bedfordshire, where we were kitted out. From there we went to the RAF base near Hednesford (near Cannock Chase, not far from Birmingham) for eight weeks of square bashing before passing out later that year. My mother said she and my dad would come down to watch the passing out parade, and my Uncle Harry brought them down in his three-wheeler sports car, but they got lost on the way so it was about five o'clock by the time they arrived. Then, in the dark and the fog, we got lost on the way back to Sheffield. (I suppose the fact that Harry only had one eye didn't help, although he served in the army during the war despite this.)

Uncle Harry was a great friend to my dad. He was married to Olive, one of my mother's stepsisters. Harry would never say how old he was but if pressed would tell you: 'Thirty-seven next,' and though he was quite a bit older than Olive, who would have been in her early twenties, he was youthful and devoted to her. He went on to work at James Neill Ltd. on Napier Street as a blacksmith, and the company eventually found him a house on Summerfield Street so he wouldn't leave the firm. One year he made my dad a hot-chestnut oven, slipping it off the firm piece by piece, and my dad stood in the Wicker selling hot roasted chestnuts. Harry liked my mother, and when my dad would be having a go at her when he came home drunk (they would have been out in the three wheeler), he used to tell my dad how lucky he was to have my mother put up with him whilst also being so good at managing the household.

Me and Harry became really great friends. He was quiet, liked a pint and we could talk in a way that I never could with my father, and he was a good listener. In later years, when I had got on my own feet and had got a nice car, I would go to his house on Sundays, let him have a drive of my car and take him for a pint. He died at work from a heart attack in 1972 while I was on holiday. I still miss him almost forty years later. One of the last things Harry did was help his eldest daughter and son-in-law build their own house in Stainton, near Bawtry. (They'd all go out on a Sunday to work on the house.) After he died, his daughter named the house Blacksmith's Lodge.

On passing out, I got seven days' leave and then went to Henlow Technical Training College to do a six month course to become an air-engine fitter, though I stayed on for a further six months. I had always been mechanically minded and learned on the old vans and pick up that my dad bought. Right from the beginning, my mother didn't want me to go into the RAF. I know she missed not receiving my board every week. When I joined as a regular, my pay was £4 10s a week, and we were told we could have a percentage stopped each week and paid to someone to save for us, so I had the maximum amount of £2 10s paid to mother for her to save for me. (I always found myself skint for most of the week.) She decided she was going to get me out of the R A F and so she continuously wrote to everyone she could think of, including her MP; the Air Ministry; Mr Churchill; The Queen, even, and she wrote to the Minister for Employment saying I would go down the pit and be a miner. She never gave up!

I was finding myself with more time on my hands than I was used to and no money in my pocket. One time I got seven days "jankers" and was put to work in the cookhouse, scrubbing pans when everyone else in my hut got a 48 hour pass. I went to the CO and asked if I could have a 48 hour pass and finish the seven days when I got back. He virtually threw me out of his office and from then on I didn't bother asking, I just used to slip off camp Friday evenings and hitch-hike to Sheffield, sometimes taking a lad I'd palled-up with, who was from London.

On one of these occasions, we found a ring on the pavement and handed it in at the police station, thinking no more about it. Catching the train back, it was usually me and five hundred just like me so the train would be packed and it stopped at every station. Buses waited at the station from which we alighted to take us the last three or four miles back to camp. Just inside the camp gates was a small brick building just like a toilet block and almost everyone would make for it. The induction we'd all had included instruction and lectures on the consequences of casual sex, and photo slides showed the results of unprotected sex. All this was new to me and then I found out the purpose of the mysterious building: inside, it was a men's toilet plus facilities for washing your penis and, on the wall, a box containing envelopes with little tubes of ointment in them for squeezing down the penis to make sure you didn't suffer anything undesirable. It was hilarious to see thirty or forty young lads desperately fumbling with themselves (to what degree of success I wouldn't know) and I hasten to add that I was never one of them.

About a month after returning from an unofficial 48 hour leave (and I always got back for 23:59 Sunday night, same as all the other lads), the sergeant sent for me and wanted to know where I'd been. It happened that the police had come to the camp on the Saturday morning because the ring we had found had not been reclaimed and they'd come to hand it over to me. So I got another seven days in the cookhouse – and I never got the ring.

Whenever I went on 48 hour leave, official or otherwise, I would, as I've said, hitch-hike home. The fare back was 12/6 and I caught the train back to camp from Sheffield Midland Station. Sometimes my mother would give me half towards the fare. When I finally asked her to draw out some money from my Post Office savings account, she put her hand over her mouth in surprise and said, 'Ah thought it were for me, to 'elp me manage.' So there were no savings.

Shortly after, each intake group had to have one of the periodical medicals. It was height, weight, etc. and everyone would be checked by the camp doctor. One of his routine questions was, 'Any problems?' Everyone would answer no. But when it was my turn to be asked, I said, on the spur of the moment, 'Yes, Sir.' His head shot up in astonishment and he said, 'What problem?' I replied, 'I'm depressed, Sir.' 'What by?' 'Depressed at being in the RAF, Sir. It's like being in prison, Sir. And I've done nothing wrong, Sir.' He didn't know what to say so put me on medical report and I knew that now I'd done it, I'd have to keep it up. This is how it went: I was required to go to the medical centre every morning. The orderly would give me two little tablets to take. I didn't know what they were and I'd let them stick at the back of my throat, then spit them out as soon as I got outside. After a week I went in front of the doctor again, who asked me if I felt any better. 'No, Sir.' A few days later the camp commanding officer sent for me. He was a group captain and his retort was, 'Look lad, why not stop this bullshit and say that you're okay and decide to put your back into it?' I wouldn't respond; I'd made up my mind to keep it up.

By then I knew that others were doing the same thing. (One of them was a corporal who had been in for a few years and was running around the camp slapping his arse, thinking he was a cowboy.) I was then sent for a medical at Halton Military Hospital where I just gave daft answers to every test and question they asked. I think, in fact I'm sure, that what swung it for me was the sad fact of something that happened at this time and was in all the national newspapers: At the same camp, Henlow Technical College, was a young lad who committed suicide in 1951. He had signed up for four years, wanting to be a radio/radar technician. Instead, they put him down for air-engine fitter and he felt he had been duped. He had gone home for the weekend on a 48 hour pass, and on the Sunday evening when his parents had reminded him that it was time to be getting back to camp for 23:59, he had said that it didn't matter, as long as he was back for eight o'clock Monday morning. After they had gone to bed, he strapped a home-made device to himself and connected it to the television. When he turned the television on, it blew his chest out. As well as being in the papers, it was reported on by the BBC, who already knew about him. He was sure that he had a future with the BBC when he finished in the RAF. (All this is on record.)

I believe that the RAF felt they couldn't risk anything like this happening a second time and so they gave me, and anyone else, the benefit of the doubt and I got a medical discharge. I had to sign that I wouldn't make any claim on them in the future. So I was now out, just turned 19 and looking for a job.

Only a week later I got a job at Fletchers Bakery in Claywheel Lane. I was supposed to be on maintenance but all I was doing was greasing machines. They were having a complete bread plant installed, and there were half a dozen fitters working to install it who came from Peterborough and were staying in digs in Sheffield. (I went out with them one Thursday night and got absolutely paralytic drunk in The Victoria pub on Penistone Road.) I only lasted two months on the job; I was a bit bolshie and complaining every week that my money was short. (About forty years later I realized I had a son who was just like me.) From there, I got a job working at a firm called Flame-Hardeners, in Bailey Lane, off West Street. However, getting paid the bonus turned out to be on a "jam tomorrow" basis and I was there for six months when they sacked me for threatening to throw the manager down the stairs.

On the brighter side, it was during this time in 1952 that I met Mary, the young woman who was to become my wife. I was introduced to her by her eldest sister, Betty, and her husband Jim, a lovely man. (Years later they both came to work for me.) I was six weeks older than Mary. She was the youngest of three brothers and three sisters, and her family lived on the Manor estate.

I decided to go back to mirror polishing and got a job at Tom Gilpin Ltd. on Mary Street. Actually, it was my dad who got the job and he asked for me. But he soon started having Fridays off to go round the market so the boss, Mr Bradshaw, sacked us both. A couple of weeks later I wrote to him asking for my job back. He replied, telling me to go and see him. When I did, he said, 'You can come back but I don't want your father.' I was, of course, still courting Mary, and Mr Bradshaw was a good boss to me at the time.

Uncle Harry and Aunt Olive

CHAPTER 10

POOR RELATIONS

As soon as my mother realized I was serious about Mary, my life became hell and the next few years were very difficult. My mother was hostile towards Mary, and she soon made it clear that Mary wasn't welcome in her house. Matters steadily got worse. She refused to speak Mary's name and would only refer to her as 'it' or 'her'. She said her sister Connie had known Mary's family some years earlier and had told her all kinds of stories, which she said she believed, even though she would say that Connie was a habitual liar about many things. But it seems Mary's father had been a bit of a handful when he was younger: known as "Mad Jack", he was related to the Mooney gang (a cousin) and had been sent to prison for being a bookie's runner.

My mother also expected me to help my dad at all times, which I did. By now, I'd decided that I had to get married to get away and I was trying to save up. After getting home from work, I would hurry having my tea, get washed and changed and go out as quickly as I could. One particular day she was really angered by this and when I was ready to go out of the door, she asked me why I was in such a hurry. I told her why and as I went out the door, she shouted after me the words I always knew she would say to me: 'Ah 'ope tha gets run o'er wi' fuckin' bus!'

My dad had bought a pick up, an American Chrysler, cut down from a van. He now had the idea of going round the big stores collecting cardboard and taking it to a firm called Marsden's, on Button Lane, that bought cardboard, rabbit skins and various other things. But before weighing in, he needed to tax the Chrysler, so I lent him £4 10s for three months' road tax on the understanding that he would pay me back from the first lot of cardboard. Two nights later I got home from work to see the pick up parked at the front door and loaded with cardboard. I asked him what had gone wrong and he said that when he took the cardboard to Marsden's, they said they wouldn't accept it until it was baled up. I asked him what this meant and he replied that he couldn't pay me back the £4 10s I'd lent him. Tough shit.

There was a time he asked me to lend him a hand with sweeping two chimneys near Longley Park. By this time, he'd got rid of the pick up for a Ford 10 cwt van, which was a bit more modern. I was driving the van (driving tests were back in force but he wouldn't take one) and we'd got the chimneys done and were on our way home. It was rag week, and the boat race was on the River Don. I was driving down Penistone Road and had just reached the junction of Wood Street and Hillfoot Bridge when three young lads rushing to watch the boat race ran across the road, right in front of me. I swerved left onto the pavement, hitting one of the tall poles that held up the tram wires. I missed two of the lads but the third ran into the side of the van and finished up underneath it. When I saw this I thought I had gone over him. His father ran across and pulled him out. He was unconscious. The police came and I had to drive one of them around for ten minutes to show that the steering and brakes were working properly. He said he believed I wasn't at fault and that we could leave. I was a bit shook up but there wasn't one word of understanding from my father, things carried on just the same way.

To make matters worse, I took Mary home one Saturday night and I had been in their house for about fifteen minutes when Mary's brother Tommy called. He was about 28 years old and of stocky build and a nasty piece of work. (I weighed around nine and a half stone.) He'd had a drink but wasn't drunk. No-one in the family said anything to him because he was known for not having any compunction about hitting his sisters, even when they were married. Within minutes, he turned on me and said, 'Don't come challengin' me, go an' get some meat on thi bones!' even though I hadn't spoken to him. (I laugh to myself now when I think about it.) Instantly, his mother was upset and started pushing me towards the door. She was a lovely, quiet woman and eighty per cent blind. I left immediately, taking Mary with me as I felt sure he would hit her. When we were outside, I thought to myself that if I were to walk away they would all think I was scared of him. I said this to Mary and decided I would wait for him to leave, so I hung about on the pavement and when he came out, I said, 'Now let's see what you can do,' and proceeded to give him a real beating. I finished up kneeling on his chest, thumping away at his head while he screamed at me to let him get up. When I did, he jumped into his car and tried to run me down, so I stood in front of a gas lamp, trying to get him to hit it but he drove off.

I took Mary over to her sister, Betty, who lived on the Wybourn, and after telling her what had happened, asked if she could stay the night. I went to work on Monday and mid-morning the young office girl came to me and said someone wanted to speak to me, outside. I went out and saw it was Tommy. His face was a mess. (His family always believed I'd used a brick on him but I hadn't.) He apologised for his behaviour and asked me to let Mary go home, saying he would stay away from his mother's.

Shortly after the Tommy incident, again, on a Monday morning the office girl came to tell me there was someone outside to see me. This time it was my mother. She said that my father, who had taken a little workshop in Bowden Street, had got some outwork for polishing and would I lend him £4 to buy a pair of felts to use in the polishing shop as without these he couldn't do the work. I had been trying to save what money I could; I was having £2 saving stopped from my wages, which were only around £10 a week, and it seemed impossible to reach £20. So I had to go inside and ask for the money from my savings and I knew I wouldn't get it back. I didn't. Also, Mary had just told me she was pregnant. That same afternoon the office girl came and said Mr Bradshaw wanted to see me in his office. I had never been in Mr Bradshaw's office before and when I went in, he hesitated before saying to me, 'You can tell me to mind my own business, but have you thought of getting your feet under your own table?' I said, 'I have, Mr Bradshaw, I'm getting married.' He then told me, 'If I can help, let me know.' This was about a month before my 21st birthday, which fell on a Friday. Well, on that Friday I got home at teatime, had my tea and then got washed. It would be about 6.30 p.m. I was stood in front of the fire getting dry when, all of a sudden, my mother said, 'Whoo, it's thi birthday, i'n't it? Tha's 21 today, aren't tha? Oh, ah'm sorry, ah forgot.' I said it didn't matter. (That was my 21st.) But I finished getting ready to go out and went to meet Mary outside The Windsor Hotel, where she used to wait for me. The next morning we went to the registry office and gave notice that we wanted to get married.

A fortnight earlier, I had gone to look at an old house that was advertised for sale in the *Sheffield Star*. I also went to see Mr Bradshaw and told him about the house. He asked if I had a solicitor. When I told him no, he said, 'If you ask me, it stinks.' About an hour later he sent for me and told me to go and see his solicitor at the firm of A. B. Thurniloe, in Paradise Square. This was a Mr Whaite, who took the details and said he would make phone enquiries about the house. He also told me he agreed with Mr Bradshaw that it didn't smell right and said, 'Don't be surprised if, when I say this is Mr Whaite of A. B. Thurniloe acting for Mr Naylor, they say, "We're very sorry but it's sold."' Well, he was right. So I kept looking and a few days later I saw another ad in *The Star*: a three-bed semi for £100 deposit. (At that time, by law you had to have ten per cent deposit.) The estate agents were Holland & Hustler in Leopold Street and Mary and I arranged to see the house, which was in Watersmeet Road, bottom of Rivelin Valley Road. I went back to Holland & Hustler and said the house looked okay but they could see I was suspicious. They asked why I was doubtful and I told them of my recent experience. However, this one was genuine so I asked how the deposit would work as the price was £1,495, which meant a £150 deposit, but they were asking for only £100. They explained that a bit of pointing needed doing and that the seller would allow £50 for it if the buyer did the work, and a mortgage could be arranged with Abbey National Building Society.

As I've explained, relations at home were at rock bottom and I used to stay out late then go in and straight upstairs to bed. This particular night, my mother had stayed up waiting for me. When she said she wasn't going to put up with my behaviour for much longer, I said, 'You won't have to.' She asked why and I told her, 'Because I'm getting married.' To this she retorted, 'Don't expect me to be there because ah won't.' Surprisingly, when I got up for work the following morning, she was already up and not only was she a bit more civil, she made me a pot of tea! Then she asked, 'Is she expectin'?' I said yes. 'Well, ah'll do what ah can but it won't be much. Ah'll make a bit of a tea.' Then she asked where we were going to live and when I told her we were buying a house, she was really surprised but she didn't say anything else.

I was to be married on Saturday 30 July 1954, and the banns were read at St Theresa Church, Prince of Wales Road. My brother Terrence was to act as my best man. I managed to buy Mary a pink two-piece and I had my suit dry cleaned. Someone told me I could hire a car from the landlord of the Red Lion pub in Duke Street for £2, which I did. My mother laid out a buffet in an upstairs room at The Windsor Hotel in Southend Road, and Mrs Dutton, a neighbour, lent her some plates and cups and saucers. I had paid a deposit of £4 for wedding photos, at Fred Knaggs in Burngreave Road, but I wasn't able to pay the rest so we never got them.

The night before my wedding, after working all day at Tom Gilpin, I still drove for my dad (hawking) that teatime. We got back about 8 p.m. and straight away I got washed and changed. My mother asked what the rush was for and I told her that Mary would have been waiting up at the bus stop for me since half past seven. After a pause, she said to me, 'Ah suppose she'd better come in then,' and to Gloria, 'Go up t' Windsor bus stop an' tell 'er to come down.' So Gloria went and fetched her and Mary came in and sat just inside the door on an old kitchen chair, waiting for me to finish getting ready. It was the first time in our two years together that my mother had invited Mary in and it was befitting that a friend who I worked with, called Harry Roper, came a few minutes later with some flowers he'd made up for button holes.

After the wedding ceremony, the hired car took us up to The Windsor for the buffet. There were about thirty family members from both sides. We received a wedding present from my brothers and sisters and an electric iron from Mary's mam and dad. But nothing from mine, not even a card, and I had just £2 in my pocket with which to buy everyone a drink. (And, writing this fifty-five years later, I've only just realised we never even had a wedding cake!)

Mary's brother Tommy turned up about 7 p.m. and, straight off, me and Harry Roper got his arms up his back and frog marched him down Boundary Road and told him to piss off. I made my £2 go as far as I could and ended up with 2d in my pocket. At the end of the evening, Mary and I walked down to my mother's to collect our coats before walking to our new home in Watersmeet Road. At my mother's house were my cousin Ron and his wife. Ron asked how we were going to get home and after I said we were walking, he said they had a taxi ordered and invited us to go with them, dropping us off at Hillsborough Baths. When we got to the baths and got out of the taxi, they got out as well and walked Mary and me along Holme Lane to the bottom of Rivelin Valley Road. There, they wished us well and went back up Holme Lane while Mary and I walked the rest of the way to our new home. We were very happy.

Around 9.30 the following morning we were woken up by

someone knocking at the front door. I crept out of bed and peeped through the window. It was my dad. I got back into bed. The next day (Monday) I went to work as usual. Mr Bradshaw came and asked me how everything had gone and when I told him okay, he said if I wanted a few days off to take my missus to Blackpool, I could have a sub. I didn't have a penny in my pocket and thanked Mr Bradshaw but told him I was going to get stuck in and try to have a good few weeks. I was up to my neck in debt as everything we had I'd got on hire purchase, and though I did my best, I could still earn only about £10 a week, after stoppages.

Christmas came and the New Year. On New Year's Eve, about eight o'clock, my brother Terrence walked in with his girlfriend Elsie. He said he'd come to say that Elsie's mam and dad wanted us to go for a drink at their house in Palm Street (Walkley). It was lovely of them as we didn't know them from Adam and Eve but my brother must have told them how things were with us and so they invited us to their home. Though my brother was only 18, he understood my situation and thought of us. He was wonderful to me as a brother and my one true friend all through those years, and I miss him so much, even though it was twenty-three years ago that he died.

My sisters Brenda (back) and Gloria

CHAPTER 11

MY BRILLIANT BROTHER TETS

In the early morning of 27 January 1955 I had to run down to the phone box and phone for an ambulance for Mary, and she was admitted to the maternity wing of the City General Hospital. I went to work, and just before dinner time I asked the office girl to phone the hospital. Almost an hour later she came to say, 'The 'ospital 'as just phoned. Your wife 'as 'ad a little girl!' I washed off and was straight up there and fourteen days later I borrowed my Uncle Harry's van to fetch them home. My wife carried her bag to the van and I carried my new daughter. I whispered to her and promised her the world; my world was complete. We christened her at the Sacred Heart Church in Langsett Road and named her Carol Anne.

My mother didn't stay on speaking terms with Mary for more than a few weeks. I was barely keeping my head above water as every penny I earned was spoken for, it just wasn't enough. I was going directly from Gilpin's at 5 p.m. to my dad's little polishing shop in Bowden Street, which was above the new Salvation Army hostel in Fitzwilliam Street. He was letting me have a little bit of the work he was getting and I was earning, perhaps, another £1 10s to £2 a week if I worked until 8 p.m. four nights a week, though I knew it couldn't last. Then a shop became vacant on Button Lane, behind what is now Atkinsons, and my dad suggested renting it and turning it into a café. So we did. We painted it out, put a second-hand cooker in the kitchen and I got some cheap tables and stools, which, I think, cost about £27 on tick (hire purchase) from Wigfalls at the bottom of London Road and we opened in late 1955.

The plan was that my dad would run the cafe with a bit of help from my mother and also my sister Brenda, who had just left school and was nearly 16. The idea was to stay open until 10 p.m. and on Sundays we'd serve hot dinners to those who stayed at the "Sally" Army and all those in lodgings in the area. I remember one of the first customers. He was totally blind, having had his eyes removed at the age of 10 months. Everyone knew him as "Knocker" because when he had lived in Barnsley, he sold the *Sheffield Star* on the bus station, but it seems he'd forgotten to pay the takings to the management and scarpered to Sheffield. Obviously he couldn't work for *The Star* anymore so he started standing outside Suggs sportswear shop, in Moorhead, selling matches, and would come to the café for his tea. Knocker's trouble was he liked a drink – a good one. When he was drunk, the major at the "Sally" Army hostel would refuse to let him stay there, so he would go to a lodging house on the corner of Broomhall Street and William Street. When the lodging house was full, he'd sleep at the cafe in a little side room next to the kitchen. My dad talked to him about selling packets of lavender or little bunches of anemones instead of matches. It was agreed and my dad would make up the packets of lavender seeds and bunches of anemones and Knocker stood with them on a small tray held by string round his neck. They split the earnings fifty-fifty and it was unbelievable how much money he would take; though the seeds were 6d a packet, people would give him a shilling, two shillings, half a crown and wouldn't expect any change.

Knocker used to frequent a pub called The Barleycorn, in

Cambridge Street. He could count money as well as anyone and he would change silver into notes at The Barleycorn. At that time, it had a reputation for being a haunt of "ladies of the night". One night Knocker was at the bar saying the major had barred him permanently for his bad habits (boozing) when one of the "ladies", overhearing him, said that she knew of a flat and if Knocker could find the rent in advance, he could share the flat with her. So he did and he said he finished up not three in a bed, but four: a blind man, a prostitute, her brother and a poof.

He always liked his beer and it wasn't unknown for him to get on a bus and go somewhere he'd never been before, get drunk and not know his way back to Sheffield. He loved going to the pictures and would just follow the soundtrack, and when the Wicker started showing French nude films, he nearly broke his neck dashing to "see" one, only to find the dialogue was in French. He asked for his money back. He stood on the Moor for many years and became something of a celebrity, his picture appearing in the newspapers many times until he died. When my dad got rid of the café, Knocker used to go to my mother's for his Sunday dinner, and though she wouldn't have him as a lodger, she did sometimes invite him on holiday with them.

I recall when one of the first Jamaicans to come to Sheffield came to the café for Sunday dinner. There was a big fight. The Jamaican man had just finished his dinner when another customer sat down at the same table to have his. The Jamaican guy moved his plate aside, whereupon the man who'd sat down with his dinner pushed it into the Jamaican's face. When asked why, he said the Jamaican guy had insulted him. Another night a fight started, the police came and arrested two men. When they got them into the car it wouldn't start so we all had to push it to get it going, including the two in the car!

Around this time, work had started on demolishing buildings in the Moor area in readiness for the rebuilding that would take place later. A gang of workers, including two brothers, were coming into the café and I used to talk to them. One Sunday, out of the blue, the brothers came to my home in Watersmeet Road. They said they were working for a man called Syd Williams, who lived in Coleridge Road, Attercliffe, and that they were to start demolishing a furniture store the following week. Somehow, unbeknownst to Syd, they had got hold of keys and gone in that Sunday and stripped all the lead out. They'd gone to the café looking for me, thinking I had a van – the lead had to be moved that night. I explained it was my father's van, not mine (a 10 cwt Ford). I agreed to go and borrow the van and go to where the lead was and they would be waiting just inside the gate. (It was Cousins Furniture Store, Moorhead.) I got the van and went to a lane behind what are now The Golden Dragon Chinese restaurant, and Brenda's Fish and Chips. It had just got dark. I pulled up, jumped out and opened the back doors. They were ready and in a minute or so the lead had been loaded. They jumped into the van, sitting behind the driver and passenger seats. Off I went, along Matilda Street, then Howard Street and on past the railway station, passing the bus station on my left. Suddenly a policeman stepped into the middle of the road, waving his torch at me to stop. I knew instantly why he was stopping me, no lights – the van had a dicky light switch. I drove about 20 yards past him and stopped. My hand went to the switch, waggled it about a bit, and then the lights

95

were on. I got out of the van and walked back to him, saying that I knew why he'd stopped me and I explained about the light switch. He said, 'It took thee a bit to stop, didn't it?' I forget what I said to that but I did say, 'You remember me, don't you? I used to give you a morning *Telegraph* when I worked delivering the morning papers. You used to come round the back into Hartshead.' His manner softened a bit, but he then shone his torch onto the windscreen. I think he was checking the tax disc and he couldn't have seen the two sat in the back because he said, 'Alright, off tha go.' I didn't need telling twice! We buried the lead near some allotments off Greenland Road and weighed it in a couple of days later. (One of these blokes was called Frank and years later, who should I find living four doors away?)

The café hadn't been open very long when, one evening after I'd finishing work at Gilpin's, I said something to my mother about "our café". She looked at me in surprise. 'It's not thi café, it's our café,' meaning I wasn't a part-owner. When I got home I told Mary and said I wouldn't be going down any more, that I'd keep away. By now, Carol was eight or nine months old and Mary was pregnant again. My mother started demanding to see baby Carol, saying she was her flesh and blood. I still kept away. A few weeks later, around teatime, an inspector from the RSPCC came to the house. He said he wanted to see baby Carol because he'd had a complaint that she wasn't being looked after properly, that she was being neglected. We showed him where she slept, in her own bedroom next to ours. She had a new cot with spotlessly clean sheets, pillow and cot blanket and it was warm and dry. She had a night-light and a little teddy bear. We told him what Mary fed her on; we told him everything, including our relations with my mother. He looked all around the house and saw for himself that it was sparse but clean (we even had a second-hand washing machine). The man said he had to follow up a complaint and kept apologising. He said he wouldn't be coming again; however, he did – to ask if I would give him the old boiler I had put in an outhouse when I replaced it with the second-hand washer. Of course, I gave it to him for someone who hadn't got one.

All this time, I was on good terms with my dad and my brother Terrence was brilliant with us. He had a BSA Bantam 125 two stroke motor bike and would take me anywhere I asked him to, and on the few occasions I had the money to take Mary to the pictures, he would come and baby-sit Carol for us. One night that he came over he was looking shame faced and was very quiet. When we got married, my mother had lent us a pair of old curtains that were so worn and thin you could almost see through them but they were better than nothing. (They didn't completely close, either, so they were held together in the middle with a safety pin.) Terrence said, 'My mother's sent me for 'er curtains, she says she needs 'em.' So I took them down for him to take and I put a curtain wire across and hung newspaper from it, like people used to do when they were decorating, until I managed to save enough money to buy some curtains.

I was still working at Tom Gilpin's. It was a Wednesday afternoon and we were making our book up for the week – what we had earned, Thursday and Friday going in for the next week – when the manageress (her name was Edna Jessop) came to me out of the blue. 'Mr Bradshaw says you've to tek a week's notice.' I was speechless but wouldn't show any emotion. 'Okay,' I said. Nothing more. Mary was pregnant again, so within half an hour I had finished the job I was doing, had washed my hands and was walking up Mary Street looking for another job. I had to find something. I went round the top of Mary Street, Hereford Street and onto Sylvester Street because there were a lot of cutlery firms around there. I went to one called Joseph Elliot Ltd., a very old and prestigious firm, and they had a card in the window saying *Mirror Polisher Required.* I went in and took the job to start the next morning. Trouble was it only paid 3s 5d per hour and I couldn't manage on £10 before stoppages (which took it to about £9 10s per week), but I took the job until I could find something better. I worked till Friday afternoon and then I went round to Gilpin's for my bit of money, my cards and my P45. The girl went into Mr Bradshaw's office for a moment and then came out and said I couldn't have them. Mr Bradshaw followed her out and said to me, 'You were given a week's notice and you'll serve a week's notice.' I replied, 'You gave me a week's notice, but you can't make me work a week's notice. Anyway, what did you sack me for?' 'Because you were greedy,' he answered. (Because I was trying to earn as much as I could.) I knew then what he meant: at this time of year orders would drop off, and what we were making was going into stock, not out to the mail order firms, which were the bulk of his customers, and orders never picked up until around the summer.

So I got my cards and P45 and after about three weeks, the charge-hand at Elliot's came to me and said, out of the corner of his mouth, 'Don't let on t' others, but ah've been upstairs and got thee another 3d an hour.' I couldn't say anything because while he was a nice bloke, I had to find something else. I was also being stopped emergency tax during this four weeks, but the following week I got my tax back, a rebate of £9, on top of my wage. I knew what I had to do.

I had two uncles who were mirror polishers, and they worked together. (In fact, they worked together for about twenty years until they both retired.) They rented a spindle from a man called George Adams at a firm called McClory in Headford Street, near Viners Cutlery Manufacturers Ltd. I asked my uncles if I could have the use of their felting machine, and I also asked George Adams if I could rent a spindle-end, same as my uncles. Yes. The rent was 10/- a week. I then went back to Joseph Elliot's, said I was leaving but asked if they could find me some outwork. They liked my work and I knew I was very good at what I did, and while they wanted me to stay, they did understand my reasons for leaving and found me some work. I also went to several other manufacturers and got a bit of work. I laid my tax refund out in work materials. Though I was a little better off, I was doing a lot of fetching and carrying. But then the same thing happened again and no orders for the manufacturers meant no work for me. So back to looking for a job, any job.

Again, a card in a window, this one for someone for polishing fish eaters at Cooper Bros. Ltd., Arundel Street, working for a man called Jeff Bebb. This was around the end of June 1957 and everybody had two weeks' holiday in July/August. I hadn't any holiday pay to come so I asked Bebb if there was any chance of working those two weeks. He said no problem. The last week in July came up and it was Friday, about 4pm, when Jeff Bebb came to me and said he had something to tell me. He took me aside and said, 'Ah'm sorry, but ah'm lettin' you go.' I asked him what he meant and he told me that was it, I was sacked and I asked him, 'When?' and he said, 'Now, at five o'clock.' I felt sick to my stomach; I'd been used. (A long time after, I read in *The Star* that Bebb's wife, who was a school teacher, had been found guilty of shoplifting. I knew that the first thing he'd do would be to move house because he wouldn't be able to face his neighbours. I didn't feel sorry for him.)

I was trying to get out of mirror polishing and asked my wife's brother-in-law if he could get me on where he was working, a firm called Industrial Painters Ltd. The gaffer was a man called Gow, a real hard boss but fair, who set me on at 4/11 an hour. He would say, 'Ah want a pound for a pound, not nineteen and elevenpence, not a pound an' a penny. Ah want a pound of work for a pound of pay.' I turned up to a job at English Steel Ltd, Saville Street, painting the steel structure of the works. The men on the job were all Irish, all been drunk the night before. I had no overalls so I tied my trouser bottoms and coat sleeves with string, fastening my coat right up to my neck. I was given a wire brush, paint scraper, paint kettle and a big paint brush and then told 'Right, get up there wi' that lot!' ninety foot, a long way above the crane track (a rail which hoisting cranes move along). I climbed up, hanging on for dear life, and working off battens which were placed across the steel trusses, scraped big rust bubbles off with the scraper, then wire brushed the girder before painting it with this red lead paint. Before long I realized the others weren't doing quite the same job so I copied what they did, which was to just paint everything without bothering with the brush and scraper. But every so often you had to step off the battens and hang onto anything you could reach whilst the others flighted the battens across to the next set of trusses. My hands were covered in this red lead paint and the brush would slip out of my hand, falling all the

100

way down to the ground. I had to watch for where it landed and climb all the way down to get it and then climb all the way back up again. Apart from not wanting to have to do that too many times, I also thought I was going to finish up breaking my neck, so I lasted a week.

I went back to mirror polishing and also got a job with the *Sheffield Star* doing early morning deliveries which started at 2.30 a.m. and finished at 6 a.m. Then I'd do 4 p.m. till 6 p.m. (A lot of milkmen did this work because they could deliver the papers and milk at the same time.) Well, I didn't last long there, either, because I had to walk to work and was always late.

I've no idea how we got through those few weeks. In August Mary gave birth to another daughter, whom we christened Marilyn. Between the births of Carol in January 1955 and Marilyn (when Carol was 12 months old), Mary had become pregnant again and we had a little boy. He was born very quickly in January 1956. This is what happened: Mary went into labour, and I ran down to the phone box to call the ambulance and midwife, but when I got back and up the stairs, Mary was already giving birth. I ran to the house opposite to a neighbour called Mrs Gillett, asking for help because I didn't know what to do. She came but I don't think she knew what to do, either. He looked so slippery I knew that if I tried to pick him up I would have dropped him. A few minutes later the ambulance arrived and took Mary and the baby to the Northern General Hospital's maternity ward. He was very fragile and at 10 weeks developed gastroenteritis and was taken into Lodge Moor Hospital. We had named him Paul Graham. At the same time, Carol became very ill and was admitted to the Children's Hospital. So we were going to Lodge Moor and from there straight to the Children's Hospital where, after they'd made a diagnosis, we were told Carol had meningitis. It was late winter, with snow on the ground. Terrence lent me his BSA to go to Lodge Moor Hospital and onto the Children's Hospital, Mary riding pillion. We were coming down Broomhill and as I turned the corner to go down Clarkson Street, I skidded, we came off, and Mary fractured her knee. Two weeks later we stayed at Lodge Moor Hospital where baby Paul died. I asked my Uncle Albert if we could bury him in his family grave at City Road Cemetery and that's where he lies. The undertakers were Reed, in Duke Street. They gave me the bill as we came away from the graveside. It was only £10 10s but I couldn't pay it, so they took me to the County Court. The bill did get paid but I don't know how I did it, and I will always be ashamed that I didn't have the money for my baby son's funeral.

From left to right – Lawrence, Gloria, Marilyn, my mam, my dad, "Knocker" and Carol at the miners' holiday camp in Skegness

CHAPTER 12

LITTLE MESTERS

I was now the father of two little girls, and money was tighter than ever but, looking back, some of my happiest memories are of that time. When I used to take them somewhere on the bus they would be looking out of the window and laughing and giggling. They were always well behaved and when people said how happy they appeared to be, I felt so proud. At home, when I would be reading *The Star*, one of them would whisper to the other, 'Let's get me dad down,' and they'd get me onto the floor, wrestling me and tickling me until I surrendered, which I always did. On Sundays I would take them out in the pushchair while Mary cooked the Sunday dinner. Later on, when they had grown up to 8 and 10 and I was working at Latham and Owen, Mary would put them on the circular bus at the bottom of Rivelin Valley Road and I would meet them at the bus stop in Herries Road at about 5.30 p.m. We'd go to the Children's Library at Hillsborough Park and then walk home to Watersmeet Road. Later, Carol joined the Brownies, going with another, older girl who took her there and brought her home after. Carol loved being in the Brownies and never missed.

It was now eighteen months after I worked for Jeff Bebb and Marilyn was born, and the hard times continued. I tried to leave the cutlery business but I didn't have a trade to turn to. My brother Terrence, on the other hand, had the sense to get out while he was still young. He got a job at Samuel Fox Ltd., in Stocksbridge, working for a Darlington firm as a pipe-fitter's mate. He stuck it out, studied hard, learned the trade and became a pipe fitter/plumber/heating engineer, eventually working for Tetley Brewery for over twenty years and becoming a valued employee and Chief Shop Steward for this part of the country (Burton-on-Trent to Runcorn). He would have made a good politician but he landed too good a job with Bass Charrington, and when he became ill years later, they really looked after him, both before and after he died in 1988.

I still didn't have two halfpennies to rub together. I couldn't go out driving for my dad except at weekends so he had to find someone else, and he had some right characters. There was a bloke with a wooden leg (I don't know how he managed the clutch) and another called Stirling Moss because he drove so slowly – 10 miles per hour. My dad used to bring him home for his tea and it was always a ritual because Sterling Moss had a mania for cleanliness, and once he got in front of the sink you couldn't move him. He'd roll up his shirt sleeves as far as he could get them, turn down his shirt collar and tuck his shirt right up. (He would have stripped to his waist but my mother wouldn't let him.) He'd wash his head, face and arms over and over again (he was bald) and then go into the front garden to the little pond we had and sit with his feet in it, washing his legs and trying to wash his feet without taking his boots off. Then my dad went into partnership with a man called Paddy Wild, who lived a couple of hundred yards away from us on Boundary Road. He wasn't very big, about 5' 6" or so, and spoke very quietly. I'd known Paddy all my life and got on well with him. He'd had a hard life, getting badly burned as a young teenager and going off the rails at one time. All together he'd done more than ten years in prison and became the barber at Strangeways (now known as Manchester Prison) when they still used to hang them. He said that the night before someone was to be hanged, there was a quietness and tension over the prison. Paddy had been given the birch and described being strapped to a wooden frame before the strokes were administered with slow brutality. As he got older he quietened down but often went out poaching rabbits because he couldn't sleep at nights. Also, he liked his women and kept himself fit just for that. (I knew him to have three women in one day.) He had a girlfriend who was married and all three of them used to go out together on Saturday nights, long before it became socially acceptable. Paddy also had a wife but he never took her out, never.

My dad and Paddy were advertising in *The Star* for scrap cars to break up but never paid more than £2, even if it was a runner. They broke up the cars behind some old shops in Duke Street, and their mate Johnny Ward lived at the back of a horsemeat shop and they put the second-hand parts in the shop window. If a car was a runner, they'd sell it on the estate to anyone they knew, family or friends, it made no difference; they'd sell them the car for £8 or £10 and once they'd got hold of the money, that was it, it didn't matter how much the buyer complained about the car. When they had someone come to look at one they'd advertised, my dad would want to start telling them how good it was but Paddy would say, 'Lol, jus' tell 'em it goes like a bomb.' My dad even sold one, a Standard Eight, to my sister's husband. The engine blew up the same week and he still couldn't get his money back.

Eventually, the shops were pulled down to build Park Hill flats, but Paddy still lives in the same house in Boundary Road. For many years he still called in to see me in Castle Market and we'd have a chat and a laugh about "the old days". Sadly, he started with Alzheimer's. I still think the world of him.

Thinking back to 1956, to the time I worked for myself at the firm called McClory (an old, run-down cutlery firm), I got back there after going round various firms asking if they wanted any mirror polishing done. My uncles said that whilst I'd been gone, two men had been and were enquiring about me. My Uncle George said they were big blokes and looked like flatties (detectives). I realized who they were: the manager and one of the directors from Joseph Elliot Ltd. I went to see them and they told me they liked my work, but they weren't happy about their cutlery going off the premises and then asked if I would go back if they fitted me out a workshop. 'Of course,' I said. They did it at a very small rent on condition that I put their work first. Well, I was there for about nine months and then the same thing, again – the work dropped off and I had to leave and look for a job inside. I decided to go to Lewis Rose Ltd. on Bowling Green Street but between times I had, for the first time in my life, become ill. I think it was flu but the result was that I had no money to come from anyone. Out of desperation I went to the Social Security office in Dodd Street, near Hammerton Road Police Station, to ask for help. I explained my circumstances to the man and he took me back to 39 Watersmeet Road to see for himself. I was eventually given £1 10s and it was made clear they didn't want to see me again. It's the only time in my life I've asked anyone for help, but I had baby Carol to look after.

I got work at Lewis Rose but I'd only been there a couple of weeks when I received a phone call in the office. It was a Mr Ronald West, who was the boss at a firm called Leppington Ltd., situated on Brown Street. He threatened me with the police if I didn't go to see him. I remembered I had done a bit of polishing for them and that on the Friday before I had become unwell, I'd drawn for some steak blades and hadn't done them, about £4.. I went to see him and he said if I didn't pay the money back, he'd fetch the police in. (He was big and a nasty bully.) I offered 10 shillings a week and took this amount down for three Fridays. The third time I went I told him I wasn't going to pay any more and that if he fetched the police, I would see he'd get done for compounding a felony, which was a serious offence. I never heard from him again and he'd already had his £4 out of me months earlier in the poor prices he paid.

By the time I'd been at Lewis Rose for about six weeks, I knew I had to find something else. I was only drawing £8 10s a week, and I was falling further and further behind in paying people, the mortgage, etc. and getting county court summonses left, right and centre. In fact, the county court man was coming so often we were on first name terms and he'd say, 'It's only a little one this time, Derek.' One Wednesday afternoon, the foreman came to me and gave me a week's notice, but I couldn't care less about leaving. (To add to my problems, I was also being harassed by a woman who worked at the firm. She was a nymphomaniac wanting me to meet her away from work. When I told her I'd got no money to go anywhere, she said she would pay. Well, thanks, but no thanks. The men had already warned me about her, and later I read in the *Sheffield Star* that her husband had stabbed the son-in-law. I had a good idea why.)

When I got home that Wednesday, Mary said there was a letter for me. It was from Mr Mosley of R. F. Mosley & Son Ltd., who I'd done a bit of work for whilst I was at Joseph Elliot's, asking me to go and see him. I went the following morning and he explained that he had gone round several firms I had done work for to get my address. He asked me to work for him and said he would find me a workshop inside. I was required to start as soon as possible and I said I would but that I had no money for work materials. He told me that wasn't a problem and that I was to get everything I needed and charge the items to the firm. I told him I would get them from Fred Jones on Wellington Street and I started work on the Monday morning. The rent was 15/- per week and for that I also got two buckets of coal. So it seemed my luck was starting to change, and my sister Brenda said, 'Right, ah'm comin' to work for tha,' even though I said there was only enough for myself. (I remembered how, when she was only a little girl of about three, she used to want to follow me to school and would cry after me when she couldn't.) But when the rent was increased to 30/- per week, I just had to find some extra work, which I did, eventually.

The firm of R. F. Mosley & Son Ltd. was situated on the corner of Randall Street and Hill Street, just off Bramall Lane. It had been a large, important company but had gone down and was now much smaller, though they still manufactured cutlery of the highest quality. This was important to me as I liked doing a good job and, of course, I could charge better prices: 2/6 and 3 shillings per dozen for table and dessert knives, or 30 shillings and 36 shillings per gross (144). And for this I had to pick up each knife five times. On the other hand, I would only get 2 shillings and 2/6 per dozen for lower quality work and sometimes as little as £1 per gross for cheaper quality. If they knew you needed the work, they would want you to work for even less and that amounted to no more than bread and fat money, so you can see why I preferred to do what was known as "best work": silver plated, ivory, stag, etc. Moreover, Mosley's used to get a lot of repair work. Their cutlery carried a lifetime guarantee, and some people used to send back cutlery that they had purchased thirty or forty years earlier for new handles and ferrules, and it was repaired without question. There were a lot of outworkers on Mosley's. All Little Mesters there were self-employed cutlers, hand grinders, buffers and silver finishers. In a corner next to my workshop there were four hand grinders, and they shared a barrow (that had pram wheels) for fetching and carrying their work. One of the grinders, a man called George Allen, did work for the Co-op. They made their own cutlery. He told me they needed a mirror polisher so I went on to see them in Eyre Street. I got some work from them and the grinders said I could use their barrow; incidentally, it found George extra work, as well.

I am very happy to think of myself as one of the Little Mesters. I still have many old invoice books, wages books, etc., and I can tell you how much I earned for any particular week going back to the 1950s and 60s. I can also say I polished the cake knife used to cut Princess Margaret's wedding cake in 1960. (Actually, two were made as a precaution.)

A bit later on, my Uncle Harry, who lived in Freedom Street, off Lansett Road, asked me if I wanted to buy a motorbike so I went to have a look at it. It was a Brough Superior, the Rolls Royce of bikes! Everything was original and it had a single-seater sidecar with a dickey seat. He told me that it had belonged to the man at the off-licence, opposite, who had died and the bike was left in my uncle's garage, which was below his house. He'd asked the man's wife what she was going to do with the bike as there was three months' garage rent owing (£12). She said the bike was no good to her and they agreed he would keep it in lieu of rent, so he asked if I wanted to buy it for £12, which I did, paying £4 a week. (The bike had only done 36,000 miles and never been out of Sheffield.) Now I was able to fetch and carry my own work in the sidecar. But that winter the snow was bad and this day I had to leave the bike on wasteland off Pond Street. When I went back for it, the bike had gone so I went to the police station at West Bar where I was told it was 'across the road' and to come back later. When I did, there was also another policeman present who was staring at me the whole time. It was explained that this other policeman had seen someone nicking my bike late on the night I had parked it in Pond Street, and when the policeman tried to flag him down, the rider abandoned it and ran off. They had to satisfy themselves that it hadn't been me and, having done so, I got the bike back. I used it until my wife had our second daughter, Marilyn, but I couldn't get my wife and two little girls in a single-seater sidecar so I bought a van, again from my Uncle Harry. It was an Austin A40, with windows in the sides, and I still had it when our third baby was born.

CHAPTER 13

UP 'N' DOWN, IN AND OUT

Towards the end of the '50s, my dad was having trouble with the café. It was always up and down and he could never open at the same time for two days running. And he used to get some rough characters in. I called by one day, during the afternoon, and a mate of his, Bob Vernon, was stood outside. He warned me against going in, saying, 'There's a bloke in there an' 'e's gettin' nasteh. We're waitin' for police.' I was surprised he hadn't gone in because he'd always said he could handle himself. I knew my sister Brenda was in the cafe by herself, and I went in through the back door to find her in the kitchen. I looked through the serving hatch and saw a bloke called Jock, who stayed at the hostel in Fitzwilliam Street. He'd had some beer and was mouthing off at my sister, so I went into the café and yelled, 'You. Out!' and before he could say anything, I spun him round and shoved him towards the open door. As he got to it, I gave him another good shove and as he went through it, a really good kick up the arse. Some years later he was fatally stabbed during a fight. Another bloke who came to the café and used to stop at the "Sally Army" got drunk one night, and the major refused to let him into the hostel. Consequently, he came across to the café and smashed the big plate-glass window, throwing lumps of paving stones through it. Then he went back to the hostel and smashed their windows by head-butting them. He got sent down.

By now my dad had had enough of the café. The worry had made him ill and he was on the verge of a nervous breakdown. (I'd been saying for some time that the cause of his worry was the café). So my mother asked me if I would go to the doctor with him. The doctor said he should go to Middlewood Hospital, where he was told he needed electric shock treatment and though my dad was very scared, he agreed to it. But my mother said she was too scared to go with him and asked me to go instead, and so the first time I took him to the hospital, it was on the bus (at about 6 p.m.). However, my dad had been told not to eat anything before the treatment, and when it was his turn to go in, the nurse asked him if he'd eaten and as he said he'd had his tea, they couldn't proceed. But it really was frightening to see patients walk through the door into the treatment room and ten minutes later be brought out on a trolley, unconscious and shaking uncontrollably. I was scared, never mind my dad. I took him home and described to my brother what it was like, saying there was no way I could bring him home on the bus like that and Terrence said to use his car. So the following week I drove my dad there for his first treatment. As early as the next day we could see an improvement in him and altogether he had six sessions. He gradually got better and my mother said to me many years later that she had never forgotten what I had done for my dad. She thanked me, which was nice of her.

I said he had to get rid of the café at any price and he eventually sold it to a black man called Wasama for £400. He gave my dad £40 down, the rest to be paid weekly. But he didn't pay. After a few weeks, my mother asked if I would go with my dad to Wasama's house, in Harcourt Road, Crookes, to get some money from him. At the house, we went up the front steps and rang the bell, and when a man answered the door, we were shown into the front room, where there was just a table and some mattresses on the floor. Wasama came in and when my dad told him why we were there, he called more men into the room. (I think they were his lodgers.) He got very excited, shouting in his own language, and then he stabbed a big knife into the table. He seemed to be telling the men he wanted next week's rent and he gave my dad some money but we never went back for the rest. Some months later there was a story in the *Sheffield Star* about him. Apparently he'd been drinking, got a taxi in Barker's Pool, ended up fighting with the taxi driver outside the café over the fare and had bitten the driver's ear off. He was sent to prison, so my dad never did get the rest of his money.

Mary gave birth to our third child in June 1960. We named him Derek, after me, and like the others, we had him christened at Sacred Heart Church. (Someone also explained why we were having all these babies.) When Mary came home from the Northern General Hospital after his birth, her sister Winnie came to our house every day for about a month to look after her, and my sister Brenda looked after Carol and Marilyn.

When Brenda got married to a man named Harry Willis, my Uncle Harry let them rent part of his house, a cellar kitchen and a bedroom, in Freedom Street, so my brother Terrence and I set-to with Brenda and Harry to decorate it so they were able to move in on day one. Later, when James Neill Ltd. asked my Uncle Harry to live in one of their houses (which was a lot better than where he was), he asked his landlord if he would let Brenda and Harry have tenancy of Freedom Street, which he did.

Brenda carried on working for me at Mosley's until four weeks before her first baby was born and she was back within a couple of months. I also had another woman working for me. She was called Irene Noone. My sister has always had a very volatile temper and the two of them couldn't get on. One day, just before Brenda left to have her baby, she and Irene were bickering when, suddenly, Brenda jumped up without any warning and grabbed hold of Irene's hair. They were punching each other and pulling hair, and I did my best to get between them and was holding Brenda's wrists to stop her pulling Irene down onto the floor. I managed to part them but Irene immediately quit the job. (She always said that I held her whilst my sister hit her but I didn't, I just parted them.)

I was slowly getting on my feet but money was still very tight. My brother Terrence, now 24, was doing well at Samuel Fox's. He was living at home and was a brilliant son to my mother. He paid for her first fitted kitchen, her first brand-new three-piece suite, a 14 inch television, radiogram and other items. Now he was getting married; his bride's name was Ada Pearson. (Her brother Mark played for Sheffield Wednesday and Manchester United.) Terrence asked my brother Lawrence to be his best man and asked me to drive him to the church, so we went to a car rental firm and hired a Vauxhall Victor as his wedding car. I could see that my mother was concerned about what I would wear for my brother's wedding. She was used to seeing me in second-hand clothes or cheap trousers from C&A so I decided to shock her. I went to Jackson the Tailor on Fargate and purchased a made-to-measure suit, and when I walked into her house on the morning of the wedding, her mouth fell open in stunned surprise. (By this time, me and my mother had reached an unspoken understanding, so while she made it obvious that she didn't like my wife, I regularly went to see her and my dad.) The wedding went off without a hitch, and it was a big day for me as well as for Terrence.

By 1963 I had been on R.F. Mosley Ltd. nearly five years and had three women and one man working for me. The man was called Jim Taylor and he was my brother-in-law (his wife was Mary's sister and they were both totally loyal). Towards the end of my time on Mosley's I was getting more work than I could do. There was no working overtime so I started going back after dark. (I knew how to get in.) I would pick up my brother-in-law and a woman called Hilda Peters, go back to Mosley's, slip the lock on the gate, go into the powerhouse and switch on the power, then cover the windows and work from 10 p.m. until about 6 a.m. This was Thursday into Friday morning. Then we'd go home, have some breakfast and return to work for about 9 a.m. (One Friday teatime I was so tired I fell asleep whilst I was sat waiting for the traffic lights to change at the top of St. Philip's Road. There was a police car behind me pipping for me to go but fortunately he hadn't noticed I was asleep.)

At the end of my time on Mosley's, I was doing most of my work for a firm called Hiram Wild Ltd. on Herries Road. Mr Wild kept asking me to move to a workshop there but it was a complicated set up: the workshop was fully fitted out but it was on a firm called Latham and Owen Ltd., which was part of the Hiram Wild Ltd. group, and Mr Owen had his own team of polishers and so had Mr Wild. The plan was I would take over both teams and integrate them with my own employees, thereby having one big team working for me. I would also do Mr Owen's work and it was agreed that I wouldn't sack anyone.

I told Mr Mosley I was leaving, that I had to go where the work was. I left on a Monday and started afresh on the Tuesday but by dinner time I knew that at least five of my new employees were useless and within the first hour one had already asked for a pay rise. By mid-afternoon I wondered what I'd let myself in for and I couldn't get rid of any of them because of my promise. Well, at four o'clock I was off down to Mosley's where I announced, 'Mr Mosley, I want to come back.' He was delighted and said, 'Good God! I thought you'd be back but I didn't think it would be as quick as this!' I went straight back to Latham and Owen and said to Jim, 'Stop back until they've all gone, we're going back to Mosley's.' He was bewildered. When my employees had left, we loaded all the tools, etc. into my old Ford V8 Pilot car plus as much work as possible, went back to Mosley's and put everything back in place. When Jim came to work the next morning, he said, 'Fuckin' 'ell, it looks like we never left!'

By nine o'clock the telephone was red hot. I knew who it was and wouldn't answer it, though I also knew I would have to go to see Mr Wild soon. But I'd let him calm down a bit first. I went to see him on the Thursday and he asked me why I'd left. I told him I'd taken over two foremen, three other men and about eight women and three of the men didn't want to work. They'd had it too easy for a long time and they thought there wouldn't be any changes. However, I felt bound by my promise to him that I wouldn't sack anyone while my instinct was to sack them all. I also told him I had taken all the work I could get into my car to put me on whilst I found alternative sources because I didn't think he would continue to give me work in view of how I'd behaved. He said, 'You should have come to me. I would have found other work for anyone you didn't want, and I will still supply you with as much work as you can do.' I felt a lot better but he still kept asking me to move back to Latham and Owen and about six months later I did. I knew that if I didn't, he would eventually find someone else to take it on and I would be out in the cold. Nevertheless, I went back on a totally different agreement.

I was good at my job and Mr Wild knew that. He was a very hard business man but when something was agreed, he always kept his word. At one point, he offered me a loan at no interest to buy a new car (if you were important to him, you could have anything), but I said no because if I owed him money I would have lost my independence. One of his key workers lived in an old house behind the Royal Infirmary, which Mr Wild used to pass every morning. One day he sent for the man (named Pete Hadley) who he'd already lent money for a car. (Wild's car park was always full of the latest models.) He said to Pete, 'I've seen where you live. Why don't you buy yourself a new house?' Pete told him he'd tried to but couldn't get a mortgage because he was self-employed, to which Mr Wild replied, 'There's some new houses being built up Stannington. Go and have a look at them.' And he lent Pete the full amount to buy one of these houses. So £10 a week was stopped out of his money, at no interest, but Pete was tied. I didn't want that, even though he offered several times, and on occasions I would row with him but I always knew he wouldn't say, 'Right, Naylor, you're out.' And he knew I would never say, 'I'm leaving.'

At my peak I was employing thirteen women and five men, but I knew the cutlery trade was dying and I was saving every penny I could. Finally, I had to find work from outside because Hiram Wild and Latham and Owen couldn't keep me going, and I decided that when I left Hiram Wild I would finish with the cutlery trade. Our home in Watersmeet Road was all I had of any value and, over the years, I had transformed it into a lovely house. (My brother had fitted central heating and we had a beautiful bathroom with shower.) I'd also pinched a small strip of land at the side to widen the driveway. We lived there for eleven years.

By now, I was almost pulling my hair out with frustration and thwarted ambition, so in June 1966 I talked to Mary about selling the house to raise capital. She agreed and I bought an old two-up, two-down terraced house with an outside toilet up the yard. It was in Burton Street, off Langsett Road. I acquired it through an estate agent called Wrintmore (in London Road) for £475 knowing it was under a compulsory purchase slum clearance order. Then I approached a couple on the Wybourn who I knew owed a lot of rent. I proposed that they exchange their house for mine – that they have the old terraced house and we have their council house, which was filthy. I would pay all expenses, including the rent arrears, and give him £150. They said okay but two days before we were due to move they changed their minds. Though we'd already got a buyer for Watersmeet Road (I sold it for £2,995), I said to Mary that we'd have to stay where we were but she said, 'No. We'll move into Burton Street.' I didn't know what to say, to leave our beautiful house and move into a poky little four-roomed house! I could only promise her that one day I'd see that she had a beautiful house, again. So we moved into Burton Street and after paying off the mortgage, I was left with about £1,400. I put around £1,000 into Tesco shares (where I should have left them – I'd be a millionaire by now) and carried on working at Wild's.

Immediately my mind was working overtime: how to get a decent house again without buying one? I spoke to Jim (my brother-in-law) and his wife, Betty, asking for their help. I went to the housing department and asked for my name to be put on the housing list. I explained that I'd had to sell my house because I was so behind with the mortgage repayments and that my family was split up, with my daughters sleeping at their aunt and uncle's, whilst me, my wife and son were sleeping at my mother's. About a year later we got a letter offering us a new Vic Hallam house on the Hackenthorpe estate and we moved in about a fortnight after. I turned it into a lovely house for my wife and children, and it was only years later that one of my daughters told me how much they had hated living in Burton Street. The day after we moved out of the Burton Street house I went back to Mr Wrintmore. He knew how I'd got the house on Hackenthorpe and I told him to sell Burton Street as quietly as possible. It was advertised in the *Sheffield Star* that Thursday evening for £275. Friday morning he phoned me at work to tell me he'd sold it and got a £20 deposit. About an hour later he phoned again and said, 'Ah 'ope ah've done the right thing 'ere, someone else has jus' been in about Burton Street and ah told her it's sold but she said, "What if I offer you another £20 and pay cash?" So I've took it.' I told him he certainly had.

My daughters Carol (left) aged four and a half and
Marilyn aged two and a half

Carol, Marilyn, me and my son Derek with Larry the Irish Wolfhound at
Cleethorpes in 1965

Terrence and Ada's wedding. I drove them to the church
in the hired Vauxhall Victor

The wedding party

(From Left to Right) Carol, Brenda's son Steven, my mother, Brenda, Marilyn, me, my first wife Mary and my son Derek. 'Mexican night' at the holiday camp in Skegness. Mid 1960s

Lawrence (left) and Terrence. Lawrence was his best man

CHAPTER 14

FRYING TONIGHT

We were living in a nice house, and I was still mirror polishing at Latham, but work was getting harder to find and, by now, my work staff was down to four women and one man. I had two outside warehouses – James Dixon Ltd. Cornish Works, and Thornton Ltd. Lowther Road – in addition to Hiram Wild and Latham and Owen. We were just keeping going and I wanted to finish with mirror polishing. I had been looking for another venture for sometime and decided to have a go at running a fish and chip shop. I looked at quite a few with a view to buying but everyone was asking for more than I could raise, and when I tried for a loan from Barclays Bank, the manager just advised me to stick with mirror polishing. Finally, I decided on a chip shop in Bradfield Road. Peter Worth was a transfer agent (of businesses) who said he could arrange a loan with NatWest. At the last minute I decided against this chip shop but still moved my account from Barclays to NatWest.

Looking in *The Star* one night, I saw a small four-roomed house for sale. I knew where it was and immediately felt quite excited so I went to have a look. It was in a little row of shops in Duke Street, near Park Baths, and belonged to the chemist shop two doors below. He was asking £1,000. I offered £900 and we settled at £950. My application to the planning department for change of use to a chip shop was granted, and I found a good firm of architects, Oxley and Bussey, who drew up plans and got them passed. Next I employed a very good builder named Ernest Pursehouse and then what I considered to be a good firm, Ernest Rouse, in Bradford, that built fish and chip shop ranges.

The plan was to open the chip shop but carry on mirror polishing to claw back some money. The builders did a first-class job of the alterations and shopfitting, and I had bought the best of equipment. I took on two women who said they had worked in a chip shop before and there would also be my wife, me and my dad. I had booked a half page advert in the *Sheffield Star* saying "Frying Tonight", and I had a 12-foot wide banner outside the shop for two months.

On the evening of opening, a man came over from Ernest Rouse to show us how to go on as I had never cut a piece of fish or rumbled a single potato before, but all he did was stand around talking about anything and everything for about half an hour before leaving. By 7.15 I realised I hadn't got a smock and, more importantly, I hadn't got a float for the till, so after lighting the pans I dashed home to get what I needed. When I left the shop there wasn't a soul outside. By the time I got back, well, I couldn't believe it; you'd have thought I was giving away Cup Final tickets as would-be customers had spread into the road. It was mad and we ended up staying open until midnight.

Following that, we didn't expect to be so busy so I went to work the next morning (after checking that more fish and other supplies had been delivered), my wife and the two others saying they'd be okay to work dinner time without me. Some time after one o'clock the phone rang. It was my wife, 'Derek, we've 'ad a fire!' I jumped into my car and drove at lightning speed to Duke Street. When I got there the fire engine was just leaving and, to add insult to injury, a man from a firm that sold fire extinguishers walked down the entry and said, 'Jus' my fuckin' luck, if ah'd been ten minutes earlier … what an advert!' I went into the back kitchen. Everything was black. In the shop everything was covered in foam, all the walls were burnt and charred, all the lights hanging down. A total mess. My one thought was to bring the builders back and get the range back to Bradford. The fire department said afterwards that one of the couplings on a gas pipe under the floor was only finger tight and flames were shooting out. I believe one of the pilot lights had ignited it. Rouse came out straight away and took back the range. That was a big mistake. Because I refused to pay the balance or for the range repairs, they said they would take me to court.

I went to see my solicitor who said I had, indeed, made a mistake in letting Rouse take back the range. He explained that had I got a qualified engineer's report, I would have had an expert witness. Well, I wouldn't pay and Rouse denied any negligence and while I'd got the shop open and running again, I had the threat of a county court case hanging over me.

I was still running the polishing shop by day and now the chip shop at night. One Friday, about a month later, I had left the polishing shop to collect some money and when I returned an hour later, the shop was quiet. Everyone except one woman had gone home. She told me that while I was out, there had been a blazing row between my sister Brenda and Jim, my brother-in-law. Apparently, he had thrown a box of work (containing 30 dozen knives) up in the air, said 'Fuck it!' and stormed off. I went Saturday morning hoping to see Jim – he always worked Saturday mornings, it was his spending money – but he didn't show up. When he didn't come on the Monday either, I knew he had left. I went across to Mr Wild to tell him I would be leaving the following Friday. On that Friday I went to collect my money. I had to pay everyone their wages, holiday pay and redundancy, etc. To get to the wages office, I had to pass Mr Wild's office, and he always had his door wide open in order to see who was coming and going. It seems he had been waiting for me because as I walked past his office, after collecting my money, he called me in and said, 'So, you are leaving us then Naylor?' He asked what I was going to do next. After telling him, he replied, 'I'm sorry you're leaving but at the same time I wish you every success. And if you ever want to come back, don't hesitate, I'll be only too happy to fix you up.' And then he shook my hand. I'd worked for him for about nine years in total and it was a lovely way to leave.

I talked with my wife and we decided we would run the chip shop ourselves. We had become friends with our neighbours Mr and Mrs Crowther and he, Charlie, became a very good friend who would do anything I asked of him, and he loved helping at the chip shop. I'd put every penny we had into it: the money from the sale of the house plus what I had saved, a total of £5,800 (but I also had a nice car, a Jaguar 2.4). As soon as I started getting some money back, I decided I would turn the rooms above the chip shop into a flat. Over the last few years my relationship with my dad, who was now in his 60s, had done a 180 degree turn: now, it was he who worked for me. He rumbled the potatoes (at least he didn't have to peel them by hand), made the fishcakes and did preparation, in general. He'd also worked for me in the polishing shop. The trouble was, there he could never keep his mouth shut and would delight in winding up the women who would then get on to me, threatening to lynch him, and I would finish up sacking him! I still went to see my mother every week and after a week or so of him being home, she'd say to me, 'Derek, can't tha find 'im summat to do? 'e's really depressed,' so as I was leaving, I would say to her, 'Tell him to be down in the morning for 9 o'clock. And tell him he's got to keep his mouth shut!' Well, he would for a few weeks and then he'd start all over again. I must have sacked him twenty times.

It was 1969. I had been working on the flat conversion and just before it was finished my mother told me that my youngest brother, Lawrence, was getting married. It was going to be a quick one but he'd nowhere to live. I said he could have the flat and that I'd get it finished as soon as possible. I had made a good job of it and the only problem was that it had an attic bedroom so we ended up having to get the bed over the roof and through the attic window. I asked him for £4 10s a week, including gas, electric and use of the telephone.

By now we had become firm friends with a man named Percy, and his mother, who lived next door to the chip shop. (Percy was born in the house in 1932.) He used to sell hot pies and peas from the front room and before that he sold patent medicines. His mother was a lovely old woman of 82, and she had lived in the house since she was seven years old. She had never been in a pub in her life but Percy and she and her sister, who used to come and stop with them weekends, would have a drink every night in the house. Percy was only about 5'5" but looked after my property like a guard dog when I wasn't there. He was very pro hanging and had once written to the Home Secretary applying for the job of assistant hangman. He was also very proud of a letter he received from a Chief Constable thanking him for helping a policeman who had been set upon by two men.

Very early on I knew I didn't like the chip shop work. Me and Mary found it difficult working together, though I knew this was mostly down to me. Neither did I like serving men who were noisy and half drunk but it was a night-time shop with a lot of pubs and clubs nearby. On one occasion, my wife came into the kitchen and said a customer had said something she thought was personal and out of order so I told her to point him out to me the next time he came in. When he did, I chased him down Duke Street with a baseball bat but he could run faster than me. I met him again years later when I needed a job doing (and many times thereafter). His name was Billy Franks and he turned out to be a lovely, genuine man. He died in June 2012.

A few years later, I went to an auction and bought a hot dog trailer, which my dad would work part time. There were about twenty trailers in this auction, all in various stages of readiness for use. When I paid the auctioneer, I got the lot number for the trailer I'd purchased and the next day went to collect it. I saw that one of the others was much better than mine so I swapped the lot numbers and took the better one. I then took it straight to a shopfitter to have it finished off. The next evening, about 6 o'clock, there was loud banging on my back door. It was the bloke who'd bought the trailer which I had claimed. He was a second-hand car dealer with a pitch on the main Dronfield to Chesterfield Road, and he was very, very annoyed. I said I didn't know what he was talking about and told him to "sling his hook" (go away). After a bit more back and forth he did. But do you believe in poetic justice? I do. A few months later I was towing the trailer down Manor Lane to the pitch and, forgetting I had it on tow, I took a corner too sharply. The trailer turned over, hot dogs, burgers, onions and buns were all over the road and the car's rear wheels were about a foot off the ground. It was a right mess and as a result, my dad lost his part-time job. I bought another one so we could carry on and my dad got his job back (which included giving the van a good clean every Monday morning) and after a short while I sold it to him.

My father was selling hot dogs and hamburgers at various locations such as Arundel (Ex-Servicemen's) Club, and Hackenthorpe Social Club and sometimes his local pub The Windsor Hotel, where he could have a pint, thereby combining business with pleasure. One evening a lady from the nearby chip shop, a big, formidable woman, went to see him, saying he was taking her trade. She forcefully explained that if he was there the following night, she would 'Turn this fuckin' van o'er with thee inside it!' After that he took to standing in town, in Snig Hill, opposite the Black Swan, Friday and Saturday nights. It was a very good pitch.

My dad's stumbling block was that he always had to find someone to drive for him (as he didn't have me any more) so it was easier to have somewhere to stand rather than driving to different spots. For a short while, he had the help of a friend, a man called Joe Birch, who also helped him serve. But Joe had a problem: he used to slaver a lot down his chin when he talked and sometimes it would go on the hamburgers he was serving.

Another hot dog vendor started coming over from Wakefield, trying to muscle in on the pitch and threatening my dad. He got a bit upset at this so the following Friday night I went down and stood at the van, talking to my dad. Around 7.30 p.m. this bloke from Wakefield came and parked opposite us, outside Castle House. He didn't get out of the van, just sat glaring at us, the reason being I had a huge, very nasty Alsatian dog with me. The next day I was at the chip shop and the bloke paid me a visit to see if we could come to some arrangement. He suggested that my dad stand mid-week and he on Fridays and Saturdays. I told him to get lost, and we never saw him again.

Eventually my dad got fed up with selling burgers and stuck to working for me part time at the chip shop. He liked the job and was very reliable but when I sold it and bought the snack bar in Castle Market, he had expectations of working there. The trouble was I already employed an old man named Harold who'd had the job a long time and I felt I couldn't sack him to let my dad have the job. My dad never said anything about it but I knew he was very hurt and I felt bad about it, too, but I had to do right by Harold. Quite a bit later, I bought another ice-cream van and my dad came back to work it for me, again. He never let me down and no matter how busy it was, he wouldn't have anyone else working in the van with him. I wonder why? He used to love counting how much he'd taken.

CHAPTER 15

THE LUCKY STAR

I had some trouble at the chip shop, again. Serious this time. It was about 10.30 on a Friday night and the shop was full. There was a man almost at the front of the queue. Three men aged about 25 to 30 who had had a drink (not drunk, but noisy) clearly knew the man and from outside the shop they started to shout to him to get their orders for them. Other customers objected to this and things were getting heated so I decided to go down the entry to the front of the shop to get the men away. As I passed my wife, who was still serving, I said to her, 'When you go into the kitchen, phone for the police,' and as I went through the kitchen, I picked up a police truncheon that Percy had given me for protection when I was going home at night with the takings. When I got to the front, the men had forced their way inside the shop. I said to them, 'Let's have you out. You're not getting served and you're barred.' By this time there were quite a few people stood around watching. The men came out of the shop and started walking towards me, saying what they were going to do to me. I was walking backwards, telling them that I would use the truncheon if I had to, but they took no notice and kept coming towards me. One chucked a stone that hit me on the forehead but, fortunately, there was no real thrust behind it and another tried to kick me in the stomach. And whilst I was still backing away, I decided there was no way I was going to retreat around the corner. (Some weeks before, a bloke had done just that and got a severe kicking and that wasn't going to happen to me.) Suddenly they spread out across the pavement and then rushed me. I went bang! bang! bang! hitting one across the collar bone, one on the elbow and the other on the head (I didn't have time to pick my spot with him). That stopped them in their tracks but the one I had hit on the head was staggering about in the middle of the road, covered in blood. A minute later there were police cars everywhere. A policeman came over to me and I gave him the truncheon, saying, 'I'm sorry, but I've had to use this.' He took it off me and told another policeman to hold me by the arm. Another officer was in the road trying to wipe blood from the man's eyes and apply a dressing and bandage to his head. There were policemen everywhere. One of them walked the man I had to hit on the elbow down from the corner and when the guy saw me stood in the shop doorway, he tried to attack me again but finished up fighting with the policeman and rolling about on the floor. My thought was, good, makes me look better. I don't know what happened to the third man. As for the man in the queue who tried to get them served, my friend Charlie had pinned him up against the shop window, banging him up against the glass. The thought that flashed into my head was Charlie, don't break my fucking window! A plainclothes detective took the man and walked him down the road, telling him to go home but, instead, he walked back, whereupon the plainclothes man arrested him. It came out later that he'd been released from prison only that morning. I was put in a police car to be taken away. The driver was one of the biggest policemen I've ever seen and when he was ready to drive off, another policeman came across and said to him, 'Will tha be alright on thi own wi' 'im?' The driver turned and looked at me, then said,

'Yeah, we'll be alright, won't we?' and took me to West Bar police station.

I was calm and polite and repeated several times that I was sorry I'd had to use the truncheon but that I'd had no choice. Whilst I was sat on a bench, they brought the three men back from the hospital to the station, and when they saw me, they started shouting across, 'We'll get tha, tha little cunt!' This was all to my benefit. Then I was photographed and fingerprinted, etc. before being released at about 4 o'clock Saturday morning. Later I was charged with inflicting grievous bodily harm and was sent to the assizes for trial. I pleaded not guilty and elected to go for trial by jury. A few weeks later I saw the sergeant on West Bar. He said I had nothing to worry about but I said, 'If that's the case, why am I being prosecuted?' He said I'd get off, followed by: 'If tha gets sent down, ah'll do it for thee. Tha's 'ow sure ah am.'

My solicitor had got me a good barrister. On the day of the trial I was stood in the dock whilst the first police witness said that he had spoken to me outside the shop. He'd been a by-stander and said that I was holding what he thought was a chair leg in my hand and that when he asked me to give it to him, I refused. I thought Christ, I'd forgotten all about him. The next witness was the man with the head injuries. My barrister asked him if he was an honest man. When he said yes, the barrister followed by asking him if he'd ever been in trouble with the police. He said no. Then he was asked if he'd ever been charged with threatening behaviour. Now he had to say yes and this went on until the barrister asked the judge if I could briefly enter the witness box to stand among the three men. This was so the jury could see how much bigger they were than me and the judge allowed it. After I had stood in the witness box to tell the jury what had happened, they went out to deliberate. They were only out for about half an hour and came back in smiling. The verdict was not guilty. The barrister told the judge I had paid for my own defence and he awarded me full costs to be paid out of public funds. I even went to the police station and asked for the truncheon back but they said no. And when the man who had given evidence against me (about the chair leg) came into the shop, I barred him. He appeared to be very surprised at this!

After the fire at the chip shop, despite making the mistake of letting Rouse take back the range, refusing to pay them anything more and not getting a qualified engineer's report, the threat of a county court case against me was finally dropped. It came about because I did, subsequently, get a qualified engineer on to it but he said he wouldn't be able to find anything wrong by then. However, he did phone Ernest Rouse Ltd. and said he was thinking of opening a chip shop but didn't have any previous experience. They said they would teach him everything he needed to know, but because they had customers of various nationalities, they didn't rely on written instructions alone and would send someone to teach him. The engineer asked me if they'd done this in my case. I said no and explained that a man dressed in a suit did come over on the night we opened but he just stood in the kitchen talking about things that had nothing to do with the chip shop before leaving half an hour or so later. 'Right', he said, 'in that case, we've got 'em.' He was right; they dropped their claim.

I'd decided I'd had enough of the chip shop business and my kids weren't happy about being left at night and were getting unruly when we were both out of the house. We weren't happy with the arrangement, either, so my wife and I talked things over and it was decided I would put the chip shop up for sale. I had been buying chickens off a friend of mine in Castle Market and he knew how I felt about the chip shop business. He owned a café/snack bar in the market as well as his fish and poultry business. His name was Roy Tissington (of Smith & Tissington) and he was a good friend. One day, pointing across at the snack bar, he said to me, 'Why don't you buy that off me?' It was a long-established business dating back to the 1920s. I said, 'Okay, but you'll have to wait until I've sold my chip shop.' He simply said, 'Okay,' and we agreed on £4,500.

For many years the snack bar had a working owner called Violet Burkinshaw, who employed a woman called Nancy as manageress. Violet had owned it since she was a young woman, when the snack bar was in the old Fitzalen Market, selling it to Roy on her retirement. Nancy stayed on as manageress.

My wife and I talked over buying it and she was quite sure she would be able to manage the staff, that it wouldn't be a problem. I went to Harry Clarke at Peter Worth business sales and told him I wanted to sell the chip shop. It was a good business averaging £300 per week and he advertised it at my asking price of £5,000. We had quite a few viewers but no serious enquiries; they were all looking for the catch – why was I selling? No-one seemed able to realise there wasn't a catch. I finally offered it at £3,500. The terms were: £1,000 down with the balance at £100 per month for 25 months, 3 years lease at £10 per week. The agreement with my brother Lawrence was that he would vacate the flat when I had a buyer if the buyer wanted the flat.

Straight away I had two serious would-be purchasers: two men as partners, and a woman who had a little chip shop in Clarence Street, near Viners Cutlers Ltd. The woman, called Mrs Wilkes, came to me and asked, 'Would it make a difference if we said we don't want the flat yet? Your brother could stay in it. When the council wants us out of our present fish and chip shop, they have to offer us a house and when they do so, your brother could have the house and we get the flat.' I said, 'Of course it would,' and sold them the business in 1970. (I had named the shop Mary's Barracuda Fish Bar and it's still there, forty years later.) About a year after this conversation, the council offered Mr and Mrs Wilkes a house on Hackenthorpe, but my brother and his wife were so comfortable in the flat they didn't want to leave, at first, and when Mrs Wilkes came to see me again, I reminded Lawrence of our agreement.

In the last week, before she took over the business, Mrs Wilkes asked me if I would put 1d on the fish, so I increased the price of the fish and chips from 1/6 to 1/7. And her fish and chips were ten times better than mine. (These days, fish and chips costs around £3.50, at least.)

I bought Roy's snack bar and changed the name to Violet's. When Mary and I took it over, we earned just £13, after expenses, in the first week. I knew a lot of changes would have to be made; the staff had done as they pleased for years. They'd all been there for a long time and they each had their own favourite customers and practises; for example, buying large pieces of beef, from Brian Ellis, to roast for beef sandwiches. Now, three pieces of beef meant a lot of fat and when roasted were only half the weight, even though they gave perhaps two large basins of dripping. When I pointed this out, they said they used the dripping for customers who asked for bread and dripping, which might be two in any one day. When they made beef sandwiches, they put two or three times as much beef in as they should and did the same with bacon sandwiches. Every morning there would be, maybe, twenty window cleaners come for their breakfast and when they had a second pot of tea they were charged just one penny. Brian Ellis used to send a large piece of steak across to be fried for his breakfast. He was charged just one shilling and everything else was put on hold whilst his breakfast was done. There were many such instances so I began to change them. For a start, they did fish and chips at dinner times and the woman who did this job would get a whole fillet of cod and cut it into pieces. When I asked her how many pieces she got out of one of these lumps of cod, she said she had no idea. I told her that in future I wanted to see perhaps 65 pieces per 14lb of cod.

Of course, they didn't like these changes and they showed it. When we cashed up, the money didn't tally with the till rolls and there were shortages, so I said only named staff should use certain tills. I noticed that one of the staff, who worked three days a week, travelled a long way to come to work. Also, she was going out in her dinner hour and always came back with a bag of things she had bought and the tills were always down on these days. When I tightened things up, her husband came in and said she wouldn't be coming to work anymore.

Me and my wife were always arguing. She didn't like being a boss or telling the staff what to do, and she had to work herself up into a temper before she had to reprimand someone. Once she threw a bucket of hot water over me, and if I talked to a female customer she would want to know who the woman was and what we had been talking about. I had always known that she would be much happier if I had a job working for someone else, earning a regular wage, going for a pint and a bet at the weekend. I just wasn't that sort of person. Though I must admit that it got to me when the butchers or fishmongers were taking as much from one customer as I was ten and at the same profit margins; I realised I was taking pennies off a customer and they were taking pounds! So again, I wasn't happy with my job or working with my wife and I knew it was me who was at fault. After making changes to the running of the snack bar, it was making a living for us instead of losing money, as it had for Roy, but nothing more: there wasn't any feeling of satisfaction.

Around this time, my brother Lawrence was finding things difficult. He was working for himself, fitting sink units and such, anything he could get, really. He and his wife had just had another little girl, so he had two daughters, and I was trying to think of some way to help him out. One day there was an advertisement in *The Star* of a stone cleaning business for sale. I made enquiries. The owner wanted £400 for the van, machinery and sand (about a ton) and I bought it so that my brother could earn a living. Lawrence found someone who let us clean his house front for nothing so we could get some practice in, and we became instant experts in stone cleaning. The following week, I got us another job to clean the front of a Co-op store, but my brother said he'd been offered a job at Stones Brewery, in Rutland Road, and had to start the next day so I had to go and do it on my own.

Just before I started stone cleaning and just after I had bought the snack bar, I went into the prize bingo business. Mary's eldest brother, a very amicable sort of man called Harry, started talking about the money that was to be made in this business, especially prize bingo. He was working for a company called Kerner Bingo and was the manager of the Roscoe Bingo Hall (formerly a picture house) on Shalesmoor. Kerner had been in the right place at the right time when the bingo craze caught on. He was a commercial traveller and went round cinema chains, renting films out. After getting hold of the Roscoe Picture Palace and turning it over to bingo, one armed bandits and other gaming machines, it was packed every night, and he made a fortune. He bought a big house out Hathersage way and sent his sons to private school.

With prize bingo you didn't need an ex-cinema or large hall you just needed a shop or an ex-snooker hall type of premises. I decided to have a go. The trouble was, others had got in earlier and good sites were hard to find, but I finally took over the lease of a small dance hall at the top of Rawmarsh Hill, just up from Parkgate, Rotherham. It didn't need a lot of fitting out, just seating, bingo blower, mike and amplifier, etc. I found a manageress, a woman called Vera who said she had worked in the bingo business, and a couple of girls as staff and we were in business! I called it the Lucky Star Bingo. I'd put up shelving in a small snack bar area and kept it filled with prizes, going to Manchester on Sundays for fancy goods, though cigarettes and sugar were the favourites. It was 8 shillings for a win, 4 shillings for half a win if there were fewer than eight players. Once we'd got a customer in, we'd do anything to keep them in – if they had a baby with them, we'd make up a bottle feed, let them change a nappy, anything so they'd stay all day.

I did a steady turn over but nothing to go mad about; there was a much more successful bingo hall at Parkgate, and I was still learning. One day, one of the partners of the Parkgate enterprise walked in and introduced himself. His name was Granville Deakin. He was a big man and a real extrovert, and everyone in Rawmarsh knew him. His father had left him a successful wholesale tobacco business but it had gone bust, though aside from the bingo enterprise, he also owned a nice little convenience shop out Swinton way which his wife ran. (She thought the sun shone out of his arse.) Well, we hit it off right from the start and I had some really good nights out with Granville, especially at The Sportsman, in Parkgate, where he was a very popular character.

Just after Christmas he asked me if I'd like to go to a trade show for the amusement industry, in Blackpool. He said it would be a good day out and arranged for a driver to take us so we didn't have to watch what we drank. He picked me up early and we got to Blackpool for around 11 a.m. The trade show was at the Norbreck Hydro, the biggest venue in Blackpool. Granville said, 'We'll have a look around the trade fair and after that it's Yates's Wine Lodge.' I told him I'd never been there and he said, 'Derek, never been to Yates's? You don't know what you've been missing, so you're education starts today!' Well, I remember starting off on vodka limes and after a couple of hours I didn't know what day, month or even what year it was. I vaguely remember going to The Lobster Pot restaurant but have no idea what we ate, though I do remember falling down the stairs as we were leaving, from top to bottom, and not even hurting myself. Granville's car had a space like a big car boot behind the rear seats and I remember him pushing me into this, but I don't remember anything about getting back to Sheffield. (I just know it was late.) Apparently, he and the driver got me to my door, sat me down, knocked and then ran for it. Despite the blurs, it was the best day out I've ever had, and we were good friends for a long time. I wonder what he's doing now.

I bought another prize bingo business at Bentley, near Doncaster, off a man called Harry Dransfield, of Dransfield Novelty Company. He was about 70 years old, very blunt and swore a lot. He was into the fruit machine and juke box business in a very big way, even manufacturing his own, and because he'd been in the slot machine business since 1927, he knew everyone else in the business and was very wealthy. He said the best thing that happened for him was the 1964 Gaming Act because it ended the 60/40 per cent agreement and brought in a fixed weekly rental. He had agreements with the leading breweries, over 7,000 machines out on rental, and employed a large team of engineers (mostly ex RAF). He knew what his income was and no worries. I talked with one of his managers who said they had bought the prize bingo at Bentley to learn about the business. Harry Dronfield then gave this manager the task of putting together and opening a group of twenty prize bingo halls, all to be in prime locations, and to show a profit at a minimum of £1,000 each per week. So his first job was to sell off this little prize bingo shop which they had learned from and was no longer of use to them. I gave him £3,000. (By now, I was doing a lot of travelling in my beautiful Jaguar Mark IX but it only did about 17 miles to the gallon, so I decided to take out a bank loan to buy the one and only new car I've had, a bright yellow Cortina 2.0 litre GT. Very fast.)

Unfortunately, around this time, 1972, there was talk of the miners going on strike. When the lease on the Lucky Star ran out I didn't renew it and closed it down but I carried on with the Bentley one. A few months on I had a call from Barry Noble, who later took over Sheffield's Fiesta nightclub, asking if I wanted to sell. By this time the miners had come out on strike and what I was taking was barely covering expenses. We arranged to meet at Bentley. He had a look around and offered me what I had paid for it. I accepted and we agreed on £1,000 down, the balance on completion and he could take it over immediately, which suited me. But he dragged it out and I had to start chasing him so I could get my money. I finally had to tell him that if he didn't complete within 14 days I was going to the council and surrendering the gaming licence, which was still in my name. That meant he would have to close down. He was good enough to finish the business promptly.

So that was that, I was out of the bingo business and back to the snack bar, and though I never really made any money from the bingo, I had enjoyed myself. I was offered more work cleaning houses and other buildings so I got on with that, and I eventually found someone to work as the manager of the snack bar. My wife was happy working from 9 a.m. till 4 p.m. and I was happier stone cleaning and running the snack bar in between.

CHAPTER 16

MEETING JOAN

Each morning I used to go up to a newspaper stall in the market for my *Daily Express* and I'd lean on the railings to read it. One morning I went up and the old woman who ran the stall (for G.T. News) wasn't there. There wasn't anyone on the stall, or so it appeared. Then I heard a voice say, 'Can I help you?' and I looked over the counter to see a young woman knelt down, sorting out magazines. It was July 1973 and THIS WAS THE MOMENT THAT WAS TO CHANGE MY LIFE but of course I didn't know it at the time. She stood up. I can still remember everything about her, so very attractive, wearing dark blue fitted trousers and a mid-blue top and showing about an inch of tummy. I was mesmerised. Her name was Joan and for the next six months or so I went there every day, not just for my paper but to stand talking for as long as I reasonably could. We both knew there was a spark between us, but I never said a word that was out of place.

Christmas came and went. Straight after the New Year I asked her if she would like to have a drink with me on the coming Thursday (5 January 1974). She hesitated then said yes. But she never came. Ordinarily I wouldn't have bothered a second time but there was something special about her and I did ask her again on the following Thursday. This time she came. So that we wouldn't be seen, I took her out to Holmesfield in Derbyshire, and we spent the whole afternoon just talking. When I took her back (dropping her off near the Hyde Park flats, where she lived), I said to her, 'I'm going to see you again,' and she just said, 'Oh, are you?' And from that day we were seeing one another every possible moment; we were doing anything to spend time together.

One Saturday morning I was going out to do a job with a good friend who was helping me. We were going on Neepsend, past the old gas works, when suddenly he asked me to pull up for a minute and get out of the van. We stood on the pavement and then he said to me, 'Ah'm goin' t' tell tha summat now, tha's gettin' in o'er thi 'ead wi' 'er.' I told him, 'No, I'm not Bunny. I can handle it,' and we carried on driving to the job. But truth be told, I couldn't handle it, it was getting more and more intense.

By this time, my wife had stopped working on the snack bar and had got a job at the Jessop Hospital. One dinner time Joan and me were having a drink in The Victoria Hotel in Penistone Road when Mr Wild and his son passed by us. They stopped to ask how I was and we talked for a couple of minutes and then they went on their way. Joan and me were just finishing our drinks when Joan looked at me for a few seconds and then said, 'Let's go.' At first I thought she meant finish our drinks and leave but she said, 'No, I mean, let's go.' Then it sank in. I asked her, 'Do you mean let's go off together?' She said yes and I must have sat for a full minute thinking about what she'd said. I was 41 years old and had been married to Mary for twenty years. However, I'd always known I couldn't live out my life with her and that it was me who was at fault, not her. But more than that, I knew that if I said no, I would regret it for the rest of my life. So I said yes, but I hadn't fully understood her until she said, 'I mean now.' There were huge hurdles and I told her we had to have somewhere to live and I had to get rid of the snack bar first.

For the next few days we talked it over and over, Joan wanting to go immediately while I felt we couldn't go without somewhere to live and that we certainly couldn't carry on working in the market. When she asked why not, I said, 'Because both your husband and my wife will be in the market the next morning and there will be absolute uproar and within a week we will both be telling our partners it was all a big mistake and asking if they will have us back.' She saw my point. I added, 'And the first time I'm out, I stay out.'

I sold the chip shop property to Mr and Mrs Wilkes (having already sold them the business) and found a buyer for the snack bar, but all this took time and Joan would get impatient with me. One Friday night we were out in town, at the bottom of Dixon Lane, and I was drunk. Joan was with her lifelong friend June, and when I tried to hit Joan, June got between us to stop me, saying, 'Nay, she's too good for that!' So I tried to punch her instead but missed. She said, 'Fuck this for a tale, ah'm goin' 'ome!' Joan left me to go home as well and I staggered up Dixon Lane and to where I'd left my van parked in Fitzalan Square. I was sat on the pavement with my back against Burton's window, in Haymarket, when Joan came back, got me to my feet and then to the taxi rank. As she put me in a taxi, she told the driver where to take me and told him not to let me get out before we got there. The next morning I remembered I'd left my van on a parking meter and dashed down to Fitzalan Square, only to find that Joan had already been down at 8 o'clock that morning to put some money in the meter.

We were still together every possible second, and one Friday night while we were out making plans, I was still insisting on having somewhere to live when she told me it didn't matter if it was a wooden hut, as long as we were together, adding, 'I've got no money but I'll work my fingers to the bone for you.'

Early in 1975 I found a house in Brinsworth Street, Attercliffe. It had been advertised in *The Star* for £1,400. A few weeks later it was advertised again so I went to the estate agents, Bricknells in Rotherham, and got the key so I could have a look around. It was a nice old house, everything original, with a bathroom and an outside toilet, so I went to the market in Joan's dinner hour and took her down to view it and see what she thought of it. I told her, 'Have a walk around the house on your own and see if you think you could live here.' She looked around and didn't hesitate to say, 'Yes, I can live here.' That afternoon I went back to the estate agents and was asked if I knew that it was to come down as it was subject to a compulsory purchase order for redevelopment. The agent said that though the owner was asking £1,400, I could pay at £2 per week. He said, 'If the council want it before you've paid it off, the owner will cancel what's owed and keep the compensation from the council, and you will be re-housed.' I said I wasn't interested in that sort of agreement but would make him a cash offer. He asked how much, I said £700 and he went away to phone the owner. He came back a few minutes later and said my offer was accepted. Now, I do not feel ashamed of doing this, though perhaps some would.

Joan and I started to furnish the house secretly: one bedroom, the middle living room and the kitchen. We arranged to meet on the evening of the Spring Bank Holiday, May 1975. And after being out that evening, instead of going home, we went to 27 Brinsworth Street. For good. I have always felt guilty about not having the guts to tell Mary about my plans but I'm sure she already knew about Joan.

145

(Left to right) Brenda, Joan and Joan's best friend June

CHAPTER 17

DASHING DOWN WITH THE DOSH

It was the first morning after Joan and I moved into Brinsworth Street and I had gone out to buy some milk. The first person I saw was a very old friend of my father's and mine. He was called Harry Hull and he was living at Darnall. Harry was a little younger than my father, and I had known him all my life. He was a noisy, volatile sort of person, very extrovert but a good friend to me, and when he asked what I was doing down Attercliffe and I told him about me and Joan, he insisted on coming back for a cup of tea. When we got in the house, he spoke to me like a Dutch uncle, saying I had made a huge mistake, everything could go wrong and almost pleading with me to go back before it was too late, whilst I was telling him no, no, no.

As I've said, I'd known Harry all my life. He was born and raised in Attercliffe, in Zion Lane, I believe. He started standing on Banners Corner with a handcart, selling fruit, in 1942/3. I think he was the first to stand there and, in those days, it was a fabulous pitch. My dad worked for Harry for about a year and I worked with him, too, even though I was only 10 or 12 years old. Harry would be down in the Fens (Wisbech) buying plums, cherries, tomatoes and other produce and he'd be down there all week, sending everything back by rail. His goods would be in one half of a railway wagon and someone else's in the other half. Sometimes my dad swapped some of ours for some of theirs if we had anything a bit too ripe and he would help himself to a few from the other side, as well.

Harry had a warehouse behind Matthews (Furnishers), and my dad and me would fetch everything he'd bought from the goods station in Blast Lane with the pony and cart. (This shows how much we were selling.) My dad would work with Mrs Hull and I was fetching and carrying from the warehouse. As usual, I never got paid; If Harry gave my dad wages for me, I didn't get them, but I enjoyed what I was doing. Harry used to tell my dad he would buy him a new suit if he had a good year. My dad didn't get that suit and when he packed it in with Harry, it was back to hawking and tatting, but this didn't stop them being pals.

For some years, Harry lived in Southend Place, a few doors below us. He'd always kept greyhounds and pigeons and used to run his dogs at both Hyde Park and Darnall tracks. When Harry had a dog running, I would go down to Harry's house for the greyhound and fetch it up to our house where my dad would bath it in the sink and groom it. He got 10/- for this. (If Harry didn't want the dog to win because the odds weren't good, he'd give it a good feed on the day it was running.) When I was about 10, he gave me the job of walking his greyhound every morning and I used to take it to the fields where Manor Park now is. One morning, when I thought the dog had got to know me, I let it off the lead thinking it would come back to me. Instead, it shot off like a bullet. I was dead worried about what Harry would say, and I went back to Harry's thinking about what I was going to say. When I got there he already knew because, lucky for me, the dog had gone straight home but he gave me a rollocking and then sacked me … and I didn't get paid, either.

Towards the end of the war, when Harry and his wife went out

Saturday nights, they would come back to our house and join us for supper. My mother would do a big pan of bacon bones (spare ribs), for which she was known, with bread and butter. On Saturday afternoons my dad would have a good drink in The Rock pub in Dixon Lane before going to Kings (Bacon Shop) for the bacon bones, then onto Sayer's (butchers) for a joint, then home. It wasn't unknown for him to fall off the bus, rather than step off like everyone else, and then he'd stagger into the house with his face bleeding. (He didn't like getting off the bus at Boundary Road because he always fell. He preferred to get off outside The Windsor Hotel so he could fall straight in there, instead.)

Around this time, he was making plenty of money so had lots of pals. My mother was always going off at him, telling him his pals only wanted to be with him because he would pay for their beer, but he wouldn't take any notice of her. (Harry, on the other hand, was a real pal.) But these good days gradually ended and it was back to hawking and tatting again, though my dad was never stuck for long before coming up with an idea.

I'd like to say something more about the kind of man Harry was. What I write is the truth and I hope it explains my respect and liking for the man:

Harry's wife was called Edith and they had two children. He was in the army by the time the air-raids started over Sheffield, and on the night of the Sheffield Blitz, he had by some means or other managed to get home. Finding that his wife and children were out, he asked neighbours if they knew where they'd gone and was told that Edith had taken the kids into town, to the pictures, so he went into town looking for them. By the time he got there, the air-raid had just started. When Harry talked about it afterwards, he said he was in the town centre when Marples Hotel was hit, and he was the soldier who went into the collapsed building and got three or four people out of the rubble. He always insisted more people could have been saved if the policemen and the wardens had helped instead of holding him back. Sadly, all this had a delayed affect on Harry's nerves and later he was given a medical discharge from the army.

Some years after the war ended, *The Star* ran a series called "Sheffield Heroes". Harry was one of those featured, telling of that night of the blitz and describing what he had done. And the story was recently published in the 'Retro Supplement' of Saturday's *Sheffield Star*. The photo shows Harry kneeling beside one of the survivors lying on a stretcher amongst the ruins of the hotel.

But back to Brinsworth Street. When Joan and I went to live there, I had an old Ford Corsair. Joan couldn't drive, which was a big handicap, so she decided to book lessons at Keith Vessey's driving school. She failed her first test and before she took it a second time, I told her that if she failed, she should walk out of the test centre smiling and waving as if she'd just passed, then take the plates off and throw them in the back of the car for people to see. I insisted she drove as much as possible and I said that she should get used to going out on her own, even at the risk of getting stopped. Very quickly, she became a good driver and so it was back in for another test. On that morning, I told her not to drive close to the kerb and not be pulling out to pass a stationary car and then back in to the kerb. I told her to drive at just under 30 mph, not at 20 mph, straight down the middle of the road, and to take two Anadin tablets beforehand to settle her nerves. After the examiner told her she'd passed, he asked her who had taught her to drive like that and she said, 'My husband gave me a lot of guidance.' From then on, she chauffeured me around and always drove when we were going somewhere together, and though she sometimes drove too fast, she became a very good and confident driver.

We both saw our children as much as possible. Joan's two sons would come over until they'd had enough of us and then go back to their dad. My two teenaged daughters, who both had boyfriends, left their mother and rented a flat together. Later my eldest rented a flat on her own but she came to stay with us for a while when things hadn't worked out with the boyfriend; he wouldn't return the key, and she wouldn't stay at the flat whilst he had a key. When she told me this, I said I would go to see him. I would return a small portable TV that belonged to him and ask him for the key. The boyfriend and a partner had a small second-hand car pitch on Attercliffe Common. When I went down there, he got a little nasty and it ended in him grabbing me in a bear hug from behind and the partner waving an acetylene torch in my face. I broke away and jumped into my van, drove a few yards, then stopped and threw the TV over the wire fence, hoping to put it through a car windscreen. It didn't break but I had got the key. (He'd also stuck one on me and given me a black eye.) I didn't think anything more of it until Joan said the police had been and wanted me to go down to Whitworth Lane police station. When I went down, they arrested me and charged me with affray and destroying a television. I tried to explain what had happened but they didn't want to know. When I went to court, I explained it to the judge and though I think he understood my position better than the police, I was still found guilty. The fine was £60, and the judge said, 'I don't expect to see you here again.' I asked for time to pay.

Some months later I got a summons for non-payment. On the morning I went to court, Joan was telling me to take the money with me and pay the fine. I said no, I'd tell them I'd been badly off and offer £1 a week but when I got in front of the magistrate he wasn't wearing it and said, 'Seven days.' So the handcuffs were slapped on me and it was down to the cells. A little later a police van took me and fellow miscreants to the charge office on Bridge Street from where a coach would take us to Leeds Prison (also known as Armley Jail). Now this was getting serious so I'm asking the police sergeant behind the counter about my making the customary one phone call and he kept saying, 'In a bit, in a bit.' Finally (after what seemed an eternity) he called me and I shot over to the desk to phone Joan at the shop. 'Joan, Joan, I got seven days and I'm off to Leeds Prison in about half an hour. Can you get down here with the money, quick?' Well, of course, she reminded me that she'd told me to take it with me, but 'You wouldn't listen, would you?' Anyhow, she got to the charge office about ten minutes before the coach left, and I was a free man again.

The house next door to ours in Brinsworth Street was owned by a family of immigrants: Zena, who came from the Yemen, and Mohammed, who was Egyptian, and they had a son, Roy, who was 18. Straight away they came and introduced themselves, saying they had seen us when we came to view the house and had hoped we would buy it. They were a really lovely family. I had to earn a living and my only means was by stone cleaning and as I also needed a telephone, Mohammed kindly said I must regard his phone as mine. I'd used it several times and left some money on the table but he said

I must not do that anymore. (He brought cigarettes for Joan, as well.) His son had just passed his driving test but had not been able to get a job since leaving school. I was able to introduce him to someone who offered him a job, and Zena and Mohammed were so happy it was unbelievable. We had made friends for life. Mohammed was a very intelligent man with two degrees from Cairo University, but he worked as a labourer in a steel works. He was very religious and his main purpose in life was to help anyone who was in difficulty – filling out forms, applying for a passport, whatever he could do for them.

I was finding just enough stone cleaning work and Joan went with me, labouring. Very soon she had a go at the cleaning herself and she picked it up well enough to be able to do the bottom while I did the rest from a ladder. The work was keeping us going whilst I had put what little money I had left into some shares in a company called Slater Walker, but one evening I was watching the 6 o'clock news when it came up that Slater Walker had gone into receivership. I had lost 95 per cent of the shares which I had paid £2.70 for. I got 12p back. That taught me never to invest in the name, only in tangible assets like bricks and mortar.

However, more seriously, Joan was racked with guilt about leaving her children and she became very ill. She had a nervous breakdown and one day smashed up the furniture and just about everything the house. I fetched the doctor who had been her GP for a long time (fifteen years) and he came back with a specialist who said she needed to see another doctor at Middlewood Hospital. I took her that afternoon. It was a terrible place: a big, bare waiting room with walls painted dark green, so depressing (and it brought back old memories and feelings about taking my dad there). When we finally saw the doctor, we couldn't understand what he was saying because he was foreign and I had to keep asking him to repeat what he said. Before long, Joan said, 'Derek, take me home.' Halfway back she asked me to stop in a quiet spot and then she told me, 'If I had gone in there, I'd never have come out. I have got to get myself better.' And she did.

We fitted the second bedroom out and Joan's two sons were able to come and stop. I wanted her to file for custody but she said, 'No. He was a bad husband but a good father and while I've left him, I don't want to take his children as well.' I asked him if he would give Joan a divorce but he said no so we waited five years and then she divorced him. My wife had divorced me almost immediately and I paid her what was a modest settlement.

Joan and me a few weeks after moving in together at Brinsworth Street

CHAPTER 18

BRINGING DOWN THE HOUSE WITH RATS

Joan was immensely protective towards me and stoically loyal. To give an example, I was once stone cleaning a house in Handsworth and I was up a ladder doing round a bedroom window when I suddenly came off the ladder. A man had come out to complain about the dust and in a fit of rage pulled the ladder away and then his two grown-up sons came out as well. As a result, Joan charged one of them in the back with a shovel as he came to attack me, and when the police came and she told them I was about to be attacked, the policeman said, 'Ah ought arrest tha, not 'im! Tha almos' cut 'im in two wi' tha' shovel.'

As well as stone cleaning, I was doing damp-proof injection on properties owned by a man called Ted Baker, and Joan worked with me – whatever I was doing, she would work with me. I did a big job at The Strines pub on some old cowsheds they had turned into holiday lets. We worked late and got them finished a day early but the owner started grumbling over the price, so I went and stood in the crowded bar in my very mucky clothes. When he ignored me, I pushed up to the bar and asked him in a very loud voice if he was going to pay up, or what? He couldn't get me the money quick enough. This sort of thing happened sometimes.

Other times jobs were just plain hazardous. One particular incident springs to mind: The Victoria Hotel, in town, had a complete refurbishment done, including the outside which was brick and stone. The main contractors had done three sides of the building but then the workmen refused to do the river side, saying it was too dangerous because it meant working from a cradle. I said I would do it (this was whilst I had the snack bar) and put two men on the job who had only started that week. We had got the stone cleaning machine round to the river side and the cradle was about 50-feet above the river. The smaller of the two men got into the cradle to start work but without any warning one side just dropped down as it hadn't been tied off properly. Fortunately, he had the lives of a cat. As he felt the cradle start to fall, he jumped, grabbed a scaffold pole and wrapped his legs around it. My first thought was that he was a gonner but we pulled the cradle up to him and, as calm as you please, he got on with the work.

A friend who worked with me (before Joan and I went together) was named Eric Fieldhouse. He lived on Boundary road and I had known him all my life. I always called him Eric but on the Wybourn everyone knew him by his nickname, Rats. He was so-called because in his earlier days he had worked down the pit and to show how hard he was he would catch rats and bite their tails off. He was big, powerful man, like a bear. We always used to argue about how much I paid him so if I told him to go up a ladder he'd refuse and say, 'Tha don't fuckin' pay me enough.' If he came looking for me in the market, he'd go the newsagent's stall where Joan worked and say to her, 'Where's that little dictator?' Or he'd call me 'that fuckin' little 'itler'. But we were good friends to the day he died and he would have killed anyone who said a wrong word about me.

One of my last stone cleaning jobs, before I met Joan, came from an advert I'd placed in the *Sheffield Star*: "Stone cleaning. Good job cheap for cash". The enquiry was about a semi-detached cottage at Dronfield and I went to have a look and give a price. I took Eric with me. The owner of the cottage was restoring it and had got a grant from the council. The job was also to include demolishing a small single-storey outbuilding to the side that looked to me as if it had been a brick air-raid shelter. I'd never knocked anything down before and I talked to Eric about it. He said, 'Piece of piss. When ah worked for Jimmy (Childs), we'd 'ave it done in couple of hours. What we do is knock out front and two sides, leavin' a pillar at each corner, then knock out pillars, an' it jus' goes whoosh, an' down. Then break up roof, skip it, finish.' So I gave the owner a price, which he accepted, and we went on the job a couple of days later.

We started work using a couple of sledgehammers, doing as Eric had said and leaving just two pillars. Only it didn't go according to Eric's plan. The concrete roof that had been resting on the pillars fell okay but the other side, that had been up against the house, stayed in place because, unbeknownst to us, there were steel reinforcing bars which strengthened the roof going into the stone gable of the house. Well, all I could say was, 'Fucking hell! Fucking hell!' When I recovered my composure, I said we should get it broke up, meaning the thick concrete roof, and get it into the skip, quick! Again we set-to with the sledgehammers and half an hour later it was in the skip. My next problem was what to tell the owner. I set off to find a phone box, trying to work out the best way to phrase it, but finding no-one answering the phone I went back to the job. I told Eric I'd got no reply and he said, "e's 'ere, 'e's inside talkin' t'somebody. They've both 'ad a look at wha's 'appened. Ah 'aven't said owt.' When the owner came out, I said that the brick shelter must have been holding the gable end up and when we knocked it down, the gable must have been ready to fall down. The workmen inside the house had a fire burning in the grate and we could see it from the outside – most of the bottom half of the gable had come down and the rest had cracked and split right up to the chimney. (And I didn't have any insurance cover.) Amazingly, the owner was as right as ninepence about it. He said, 'The building surveyor's seen it,' (from North Derbyshire County Council) 'and he's going to increase my grant by another £10,000 to cover it.' Afterwards, Eric said, 'Tha should 'ave seen thi fuckin' face, it went white, then red, green, yellow. Ah thought tha were goin' t' be fuckin' sick!'

Eric didn't mess about. One night we went to The Napoleons Casino and a doorman pulled a knife on him. Eric took it off him and the manager sacked the doorman and offered his job to Eric. He was also a tyrant at home. He put a shower on his back door so that his eldest son could shower when he came home from work before going in the house to have a bath, and he was spotless in his own habits, doing his own washing because he said his wife didn't get it clean enough. He used to like white jeans and sweater and wore a little kerchief around his neck, and he had a chow dog that was white. When he went into The Windsor pub, they used to call him "the Fairy Snow man". Not to his face, of course.

The only thing I didn't like Eric for was that he used to hit his wife and I told him so and I said it was his own fault when, some years later and the kids had grown up, she left him. He tried a few times to get her back because he couldn't stand living on his own. But he developed heart problems (angina) and when he'd be telling me about it I never believed him and I'd say so. (He was about 10 years older than me.) It was some years later, when Joan and I were trading in the market, we heard news of Eric.

It was a particularly snowy winter. Joan and I went to work on a Saturday morning and Graham Shaw, who had a snack bar, shouted across to me, "as tha 'eard about that pal o' thine?' I asked, 'What about him?' He shouted back, "e's dead.' I couldn't believe it, I thought he was so big and fit and strong. I found out what had happened: Eric was last seen clearing the snow off the front of his house at gone 10 p.m. He then went inside and made himself a sandwich and a pot of tea. When he was found the next morning, by his grandson, the television was on and the gas fire turned up full, the sandwich and pot of tea still beside his chair. He had had a massive heart attack. I lost a very special friend.

There is much to remember concerning Eric. I recall when his eldest daughter had come to work for me as a "Saturday girl". The son of the owner of the fruit stall next to me started taking her out, but Eric wouldn't let him into the house and went down to the market looking for him, carrying a big kitchen knife. Fortunately, other lads told Martin that Yvonne's dad was looking for him and he got out of the way. Eric went to the stall, asking for Martin. When his father, George, asked why he wanted him, Eric said, 'Because ah'm goin' t' kill 'im.' George asked Eric how many others he'd killed and when Eric told him none, George said, 'Well, tha's not very good at killin' people then, is tha?' Eric didn't know what to say to that and went off home. I tried to point out to him that he was in the wrong but he just said, "e can come int' house when they're engaged and not before.' I told him, 'Don't be surprised if he tells you to stuff your house because I would.' Some years later Martin and Yvonne got married, and Martin and his brother, Ian, inherited their father's business, Bingham & Brown. Fruiterers Ltd.

Once when I was cleaning a big house up Loxley for Ted Baker, I got Bunny and Eric working with me. Ted Baker, who was a really hard man, asked for a price to clean a wall round the garden, which was very big, but when I gave him the price, he said it was too much. I left Eric and Bunny to finish off whilst I went to meet Joan and after I'd gone he asked the two of them to do the wall, which they did. And Eric told me this himself: that evening he went up to Ted Baker's house to be paid. (Baker never had anyone go to his house.) He knocked on the door and when Baker's wife answered it, he asked for Ted. Ted was in the bath and shouted to Eric, 'What dost tha fuckin' want?' Eric shouted back that he'd come to be paid for cleaning the wall and Baker came to the door, shouting, 'Nobody comes to my fuckin' 'ouse. Tek that and fuck off!' and he shoved £1.50 into Eric's hand and slammed the door. Eric told me, 'Ah never got a chance to say owt! It cost me £1.50 fuckin' taxi fare an' Bunny wants 'alf of it!' He thought I should sympathise with him. Instead, I said, 'Serves you right. Now, I'll have that for your using my sand and my machine,' and I stopped it out of what I was paying him. (I always paid him in £1 notes so that it looked a lot.)

I did a lot of work in Barnsley town centre for the Barnsley British Co-op. They were first-class payers. My first job for them was their main office block, about 200-foot frontage. I used to give them a fixed price plus the scaffold charge. (I used a firm called Palmers Scaffold Ltd.) I ordered the scaffolding, which would go onto the job on the Friday and would be erected on the Saturday and Sunday, ready for me to start work on Monday. But come Monday, no scaffolding. The caretaker told me he had seen men who he thought were workmen there to erect it early Saturday morning. In fact, they were stealing it, £7,000 worth, and I had to arrange a second lot.

Later on the Co-op gave me another job, the electrical department. It was all stonework which had been painted over and over. They wanted me to get the paint off and then clean the stone. I said yes I could do that and hired a type of burner used for burning the yellow lines off roads. Unfortunately, the guttering of the building was plastic and it all melted and collapsed with the heat, but I continued and got the job done. The next day, when I went over to collect the compressor, the caretaker said that during the night they'd had a fire. Apparently, some birds' nests under the eaves had mysteriously started smouldering and then burst into flames. No-one ever asked me any questions and they kept finding me work. They were a good company to work for and paid promptly.

(I also recall when I was cleaning a pub, the Red Lion, at Thorpe Hesley. There were some gypsies having a go at stone cleaning and so they came over to talk and have a look at my equipment. I had a helmet with an air supply, the proper equipment for the work. I had a look at theirs – they had a rubber bucket to put over the head, with a square cut out of the front to see through!)

CHAPTER 19

TAKING A STAND

The first twelve to eighteen months in Brinsworth Street were hard. I had lost most of the money left over from the sale of the snack bar and the chip shop property and I still owed Nat West Bank, though I had guaranteed Mary's new car before I left, and my own overdraft. (At one point, I was having callers from the bank coming round at 7 or 8 o'clock in the evening.) I still had a few shares, which the bank was holding, but their value had fallen. Finally I went to see the manager but it ended in a blazing row and I walked out. About an hour later, when I had cooled off, I phoned him because I knew it was no good arguing. Upon agreement I would sell most of my shares if we divided the proceeds equally; the bank would be repaid 95 per cent of what I owed and I, hopefully, would have enough left over to start a new venture. I did clear my debts, in full, a few months later.

For the next few months I kept going with stone cleaning. Whenever I had a job that was complicated I would fetch Eric. He had a great sense of humour but sometimes he would go a bit too far. I had got a job on Garden Street, an old chapel that was now a printing firm. We took the compressor on the job on the Saturday morning in readiness for Monday. We were parking it on some wasteland opposite a firm where some of the employees were working Saturday morning when one of them came across, saying we couldn't leave it there. This bloke only had one arm and Eric said

162

to him, 'If tha don't fuck off, ah'll pull t'other fuckin' arm off!' Eric was also a womaniser. I was cleaning the front of a firm called Dewire Ltd., at the bottom of Spital Hill, and Eric was labouring for me. There was an elderly woman walking down the other side of the road and he went across and stopped her and asked her for a dance. Before she knew what was happening, he was dancing with her in the road with all the traffic at a standstill. And when we were cleaning a big stone house on Montcrieffe Road in Nether Edge, Joan came up in a taxi to see me in her dinner break. When she got out of the taxi, she stood talking to the driver for a couple of minutes before Eric went across and told the driver, 'Ey, she's wi' 'im', meaning me, 'so fuck off, or else!' Joan then told Eric it was someone she used to go to school with.

Before I met Joan, me and Eric and two others used to spend Sunday dinner times at various working men's clubs which would have a striptease on. Two or three weeks after I met Joan, she asked me what I would be doing on the coming Sunday. I told her me and Eric were going to Walkley Club striptease and she said, 'Oh no you're not, lad, there's no more of that for you! If you want to see a striptease, I'll do a striptease for you, okay?' Eric still used to phone me, saying, 'Can tha get out for an hour tonight? Tell 'er we're goin' t'ospital to see our Ivan,' (his son who had broken his leg footballing). So he came down and whilst he was waiting for me, he washed the pots, washed round the sink and then set-to and washed my car, even though it was an old banger, saying, 'We're not goin' in that fuckin' thing!' (He really had a mania for cleanliness.) Then, out of the blue, Joan came downstairs ready to go out. I asked her where she was going and she said, 'I'm going with you. You don't think I'm letting you two go out by yourselves, do you?'

Whilst I was getting by with the stone cleaning, I was looking for something else to do on a regular basis. On Attercliffe Road, near Banners Store, there was an old herbal medicine shop. Several times I spoke to the old man who owned the business, asking if he wanted to sell. Eventually, Christmas 1976, he said yes and I offered him £900 lock, stock and barrel. He accepted. The shop belonged to Smith's Brewery but by the time it came to changing hands, I only had £600 to give the old man so we agreed on my paying the remaining £300 four weeks later. When Joan and I took it over we intended turning it into a fruit and veg shop but whilst we were having a sale on all the stock, some of which was years old, we thought the place had more promise as a sweets and cigarettes shop, which Joan had experience of, and decided upon this instead. I got Eric to come and help me start changing the interior of the shop as he was very good at DIY and I managed to get the £300 for Jim. (Jim used to stay open until 9 p.m. and was taking £300 per week.) Very soon we introduced cut-price cigarettes as well as branded quality chocolates, and greeting cards, and I was selling flowers on the front on Saturdays and Sundays. For six days we opened till 10 p.m. and on Sundays till 6 p.m.

We were soon taking £2,000 per week but at reduced margins. We stocked a lot of cigarettes and couldn't afford insurance, but we had two good Alsatian dogs, one of which I had bought to look after Joan when we went to live at Brinsworth Street, the other being my dog whilst I lived at Hackenthorpe. We kept them at the shop. Joan was genuinely an animal lover. Our first Christmas at the shop was 1977, and I asked her what she would like as a present. She said she'd like a little dog for company when she was on her own on Sundays, so I bought her a long-haired, miniature dachshund. He really loved her and she used to take him everywhere she went. We had him until he died of old age at thirteen.

At the same time, I had the ice-cream van on Banners Corner, selling Granelli's ice cream. This was a good pitch, a steady little earner. There was already an ice-cream van standing there on Saturdays, Truffelli from Hillsborough, and he didn't take kindly to my competing for the pitch. However, because I lived in Attercliffe, I considered him an outsider and I was getting on the pitch, middle of the night, ready for Saturdays. There was only room for one van (and the handcart for the fruit man) between the double yellow lines in front and behind, so I put four spots of white paint marking where my wheels needed to be. When Truffelli's van came at 8 a.m. they had to park opposite me. Mr Truffelli came to see me, suggesting some sort of agreement – I stand Monday to Friday, he'd have Saturdays, which was the best day by far. I told him to get lost. He made a few threats but it made no difference.

Some months later, I went round to our shop on a Sunday morning to find council workers renewing the yellow lines on Attercliffe Road and the side roads alongside Banners. I recognized the bloke in charge (he came off the Wybourn), and I asked him if he would go a bit further up the road, on Banners' side, with his yellow lines. He replied, 'If ah get found out, ah'm in big trouble.' So I asked him to sell me a tin of the yellow paint and he said, 'Ah don't know 'ow many tins there are ont' lorry so ah wouldn't know if ah were one short.' I pushed a fiver into his hand and went across the road and helped myself to a tin of paint, about a gallon, which I left in our shop. Dashing back home, I found a broad paintbrush and two lengths of wooden floor board before going back to the shop to get the paint. I went to where the new yellow lines finished on Banners' side – I think it's called Shortridge Street – and proceeded to extend the new yellow lines up this street, on the left-hand side, for about another 40 foot. By this time the council workmen were well down Attercliffe Road so they didn't notice me and because all the lines were freshly painted, mine looked exactly the same as the legal ones. Therefore, the following Saturday my van was on its regular spot and though the competition was still on the other side of the road, he was 40 foot further up it. He stopped coming and every time those lines are renewed, they go over mine, as well.

By 1979 I could see the area going down: steelworks closing, redundancies, the knock-on affects, and I knew it was time to sell the shop, and so I said to Joan, 'There's a time to buy and a time to sell. It's time to sell.' At first she said no but I could see she was looking at what was happening and a few weeks later she said, 'I think you're right.' I went to see my friend Ian Hillier, in Paradise Square, who was in the property business and asked him to sell it for me. He advertised it at offers over £4,500. We only had two enquiries, the second from a man who owned a sweet shop on Abbey Lane. Ian phoned me and said "our friend" had offered £4,750. I told him to take it. It took a few weeks to get transfer of tenancy and the new owner took it over on a Sunday, after stocktaking. As we walked away that Sunday morning, Joan was in tears. She said she knew I was right about selling but she'd been so happy there, even though it was only for three years. (And we had taken the turnover from £300 a week to nearly £4,000 Christmas week 1979.)

My dad had been standing on Banners Corner for me in the ice-cream van. He was still working in the van the week after the shop was sold and he came rushing over to Brinsworth Street on the Saturday saying that Banners was closing and everyone had been given notice. I said, 'Christ, if this had happened a week earlier that bloke would never have bought the shop!' I certainly wouldn't have, in his place.

The Old Chocolate Shop can be seen next door to the Horse and Jockey pub, Attercliffe. This was the old herbal medicine shop we bought and turned into a sweets and cigarettes shop

My ice-cream van (right) opposite Banners, Attercliffe, before I extended the yellow lines on the other side of the road

CHAPTER 20

THE BREADCAKES SAGA

I didn't know what to do next. I'd had enough of stone cleaning, and I was beginning to worry about the dust going to my chest, so I advertised the equipment in *Exchange and Mart* and sold it to someone in Cornwall. My dad was still standing with the ice-cream van for me, and I decided to have two "Stop Me and Buy One" tricycles made (in Scotland). They cost me just over £800 and I hired a van to go and collect them. (I was buying my ice cream from Granelli, and lollipops, etc. from Hulleys in Ecclesfield.) I thought I'd try one bike in Rotherham town centre and the other outside Castle Market. My son, Derek, would work the one in Rotherham square (where the church is). The idea turned out to be brilliant. My son sold more than 1,600 ice creams and lollipops in one day and I had a good day in Exchange Street. However, officialdom obviously didn't want me there and was determined to drive me out, but I wasn't expecting harassment to be as bad as it was, mainly from the councils in both Rotherham and Sheffield, and every day officials were there, having found some by-law to quote or write to me about.

Peter Granelli was a very intelligent man and well versed in law. Whenever he had the offer of a good deal (chocolates, Easter eggs, etc.) he would ask me if I was interested in joining in. He had two sisters: Rosita, who ran the ice cream side, and Irene, who ran the market stalls. (Irene was a very attractive blonde who reminded me of Diana Dors.) Peter borrowed one of the bikes from me to stand just inside Walsh's department store entrance but, eventually, he was driven out as well. (Today I think the bikes would be welcomed with open arms.)

A little later, in 1980, I learned that the CWS (Co-Operative Group Ltd.) were developing a shopping mall at Hillsborough Shopping Centre in Middlewood Road. I talked with Ian Hillier and he wrote on my behalf applying for the tenancy of a small kiosk there. Because Peter Granelli had a very successful and substantial business in Sheaf Market I had talked to him about the possibility of selling loose biscuits. He gave me good advice and was most helpful in getting started – valuable contacts, what sold and what didn't, that sort of thing. I've always been good friends with the whole family, as was Joan, and if they couldn't do someone a good turn, they wouldn't do them a bad one. But now Joan pointed out to me that I was trying to do too many different ventures and that I should concentrate on one thing and put all my (our) efforts into it. I could see the sense in what she said and we very soon had a good little business. I also bought a second-hand soft ice-cream machine off Tony Manfredi, and I sold my ice-cream van to my dad.

When the kiosk next to ours in the Hillsborough mall became vacant, the CWS were happy to let us take it over, and I got busy joining the two kiosks into one, with the help of joiners and electricians on site. With expansion to a 32-foot frontage, we now had a good business selling sweets, chocolates, cakes, ice cream and biscuits. Then Ian Hillier contacted me to say that he'd heard on the grapevine that a business selling sweets and biscuits was for sale in Castle Market and would we be interested? Yes, we would! Its trading name was Punch Stores and the owners were an elderly couple who wanted to retire. I made enquiries and I could see that it had a lot of potential. The couple wanted £25,000 and we started negotiations to buy. The plan was that my brother Lawrence would come in as a "sleeping partner" owning 33 per cent, thereby helping to raise a bank loan of £20,000. But all of a sudden the owners changed their minds, deciding to sell to another party, instead.

The following year Ian Hellier phoned to ask me if I would still be interested in buying Punch Stores. I thought about it for a few days, then said I would but not at £25,000. There had recently been a rent increase so I offered £20,000 and we finally settled at £21,250. The owner was a most unreliable person to do business with but, finally, it was ours. I gave him the cheque on the following Friday afternoon at 4 p.m., but when he went to shake my hand I refused as he had messed me around so much and telling him I didn't want to shake his hand, left it at that.

Joan was magnificent. On the Monday morning she went onto the stall for the first time, on her own, and introduced herself to the six staff, all of whom had been there for a long time. (She said afterwards that her stomach had been churning but she didn't let her nerves show.) Once again I was teaming and ladling the money (and I was driving around in an old 5cwt van with a front wheel threatening to come off). Meanwhile, Joan was enjoying the challenge and I couldn't wish for a better partner. We had always worked well together and we always did. I knew she would lay down her life for me and work with me till she dropped.

I first started by trading with the same baker as Peter Granelli. We built up a pretty decent trade but gradually it got to be that on Fridays and Saturdays, which were our busiest days, we would be

171

waiting for deliveries of breadcakes and customers were stood waiting for ten to fifteen minutes for the next batch to arrive. I eventually told my brother that it was time to start baking our own. It was the biggest mistake I ever made.

In 1986 we leased a new commercial unit in Rotherham's Enterprise Zone. So no rates for three years. I didn't realize at the time, though, that the plan was too big. We were invited to apply for a grant from the Trade and Industry Board: £3,000 for every job created. We said we thought we could create 6 jobs, that is, £18,000. We started fitting the unit out. The rent would be £1,500 per quarter (£6,000 per annum). Then we were invited to create 10 jobs and re-apply for £30,000. The business had to run for two years. If it didn't, you had to pay back the grant.

We got the money and I spent it all on second-hand machinery. BIG MISTAKE. My plan was that we would bake all we needed for ourselves at the market and Hillsborough and wholesale the rest. But the reality was different. First, the machinery kept breaking down. Second, the wholesale customers wanted everything for nothing. Third, the staff (all men) wanted paying in the hand and were all unreliable. They were also robbing us blind of stock, materials, money. Fourth, my brother Lawrence was sick and tired of being called out in the middle of the night to fix the breakdowns. It was very fortunate that he was a good engineer; I don't know what I'd have done, otherwise.

We limped on like this for a few months short of two years before I finally brought in an independent accountant to look at the figures and see where we stood. At the same time, I asked my son, who worked on the railways but was desperate to find another job, to work at the bakery for a month. He was to work nights alongside my other staff to see what was going on and then give me his conclusions. Meanwhile, the accountant said that for the last ten weeks we had lost over £2,400 (working out at £242 each week). When my son told me his findings, he said, 'Dad, my advice is to close it down immediately, even though ah'll be puttin' myself out of work.' That was on a Sunday. I went to see my brother Lawrence and told him all this and he said, 'What are we goin' to do, then?' My reply was, 'I'm going down there in the morning and I'm giving them all two weeks' notice and back-dating it by one week, meaning they finish on Friday. Then I'm going to find a baker to supply me.' Which is what I did. We had lasted 22 of the 24 months, in terms of the condition of the grant.

I went to a firm of auctioneers called Saxton, on Bank Street, to auction off everything we had. This was around September 1988. It was explained to me that if we left it any later, it would be close to Christmas and the chances were that everyone would be too busy with the Christmas trade to attend the auction. Time was of the essence, so I informed all our suppliers of what we planned to do. We cleaned all the machinery to realize a better price and the sale was held four weeks later, though I didn't attend. Everything was sold, right down to the bucket and brush. Then I sat down and listed every creditor, how much we owed them and how much the sale had realized. I prepared a balance sheet, copied it and went to every creditor giving each a copy and asking if they would accept 10 per cent less on condition they were paid within fourteen days. I had a lot of new stock from one supplier so I asked him to take it back and deduct the value from what I owed. He said yes. I took it back to

Preston, personally, and two days later he sent me a lovely letter thanking me for, as he put it, the full and frank manner in which I had conducted myself. Another of the creditors was a company called Initial Towel Supply Ltd. The boss was a lady, and when I went to see her, I told her the situation and that it meant making my own son redundant. She thanked me and wished me well. She also said, 'If your son would like to come and see me, I will find him a job.'

Everyone, without exception, accepted my terms and all were paid within six weeks. I had spoken to my bank manager and converted my overdraft into a business loan and this was repaid within three months instead of two years. It was important to me that if I ever saw one of my erstwhile creditors again, I could look them in the eye and not have to look down. Still, as my brother said, NEVER AGAIN.

Almost immediately, I found a small baker. I'd been driving around and every time I saw a small bakery shop I would go in and buy a dozen breadcakes to sample. Then I remembered that some time previously I'd seen an advertisement in the *Sheffield Star* placed by a small wholesale baker seeking customers. I traced him to a little shop in Chaucer Road, Parson Cross, and I went to see him. His name was, let's say, Paul M. At the time he was selling sandwiches to school kids and baking bread for the local people, but his products were just what I was looking for, so I asked him if he would like to bake some breadcakes for me. He asked me how many and I said about 200 dozen and though he said okay, he didn't seem all that bothered. However, he delivered them the next morning and we put them on the counter alongside some breadcakes I'd got from elsewhere as a stopgap. Well, everyone wanted the new baker's breadcakes, and each day our order went up and up. The following Tuesday, very satisfied, I went to see him to give him his cheque. Straight away he started to tell me his plans. He was stopping selling sandwiches, changing the bakery around, getting another oven and so on. I said, 'Whoa, hold on a minute, when I first came to see you your attitude was "I'm not really bothered." What's changed?' He replied, 'Ah'd 'eard about these big orders before an' ah thought, ah'll believe it when ah see it.' And now he'd got one. As well as supplying Punch Stores in Castle Market, he was supplying our Hillsborough outlet and the two were averaging 7,000 dozen breadcakes per week. He was a first-class baker; his breadcakes were beautiful and we had queues all day, every day. (I always paid him on the dot; I would receive his invoice on the Monday morning and pay him by cheque by Wednesday morning.)

When I first met Paul he was living in a little terraced house in Fox Street, Pitsmoor. Within six months he moved into a three-bedroomed semi in Shirecliffe. He got two new delivery vans, a Mercedes car, and a Mercedes wagon for his son plus a Sierra Sapphire for his wife. Next he moved into a stone-built house up Minto Road, Hillsborough, before selling the semi. By now he had been supplying me for about three years and, over time, he got further and further into debt, eventually coming to my house at 8 o'clock in the morning for a cheque and taking it straight to the bank. I was trying to advise him and guide him in business; after all, it was in my interests as well as his that he didn't go under, but he wouldn't listen. I started looking for another supplier.

Finally, he did go under. He was bankrupt and the receiver moved in. I found another baker, a good one, but not as good as him, and only now do I realize what I should have done: I should have approached the receiver and purchased everything whilst it was in situ (I think I could have bought everything for around £8,000) and then rented it back to Paul M on condition that he baked only for me.

Just after taking over Punch Stores in 1981, when we started selling our own bread cakes, another trader objected to this and whilst I didn't know who it was, I went to see my local councillor. Seeking his help, I showed him that my user clause included breadcakes. He discussed it with the market's superintendent and the result was that I could continue to sell breadcakes, and I was given consent to sell ice cream, as well. Also, at Hillsborough the anchor tenant, Presto supermarket, raised objection to my being there, saying that they had spent a considerable sum of money in fitting out their store to a high standard and I was lowering the tone of the whole mall. I organized a petition telling the public what this supermarket was trying to do. Within a week I'd got over 3,000 signatures and took the petition to top management at CWS in Manchester. I was told I must try to get along with other tenants; however, I was just as important in their eyes as a national group and, if need be, management would come down on them, as they would me. I was told I'd be given their decision within 24 hours. The next morning the top man phoned me and said, 'Carry on.'

Within twelve months we had built up a solid and successful business. However, the following year a new market superintendent was appointed to run Castle Market and secure an increase in rents for the treasury. The new man's name was Malcolm Prince and he had come from Leeds Market, where he'd had a reputation for being ruthless, a real hard man. (I think he took a disliking to me at our first meeting.) I'd gone upstairs to ask if I could put shutters around our stall instead of just curtains. We talked about the pros and cons before he said no, and as I was about to leave his office, he brought up the subject of our selling breadcakes and the anonymous letter from the stall holder who had objected the year before. I explained that my councillor had spoken to the market's previous superintendent and it had been settled in my favour. He asked if I had got this in writing. I said no, his word had been good enough. He told me he wouldn't be bound by anything his predecessor may have said and gave me 28 days to stop selling breadcakes, so I went to see my solicitor, Vincent Hale, and told him about the conversation. Vincent took down a copy of the *Oxford English Dictionary* and looked up the word "cake". It was defined as a small, flattish lump of dough. Since my user clause said "cake", he told me, 'You've got nothing to worry about.'

It was only a matter of weeks before I received a letter stating that I had 28 days to stop selling breadcakes or else I would be out of the market. Vincent Hale told me, 'Carry on. If you stop, even for just one day, you've lost.' So I did carry on but I also went to see Councillor Frank Prince, explaining the situation and asking for his help, again. He arranged a meeting between himself; Councillor Frank White (Chairman of the Markets Committee); Malcolm Prince; Jack Christopher (Assistant Market Superintendent); myself and my brother Lawrence. However, it wasn't so much a meeting as a long tirade of personal abuse from Malcolm Prince against me whilst the others sat in shocked silence. And though he'd only met me once before, he called me a confidence trickster and said I was a shark who should be up High Street with all the other sharks, and that I was a bad tenant who shouldn't be in the market. He carried on in a similar vein until we walked out. My brother said afterwards, 'Derek, if 'e'd 'ad a gun 'e would 'ave shot tha!' But I still carried on selling breadcakes.

On 31 March 1986 every traders lease expired, including mine. The council informed me that they wouldn't be renewing my lease and would oppose any application to the courts for a new one. Meanwhile, they refused to accept any rent from me. At our first meeting, Mr Prince had explained to me that he had done this in the past with other tenants in Leeds Market and eventually they had given up, handed in their keys, and walked away. He said that crocodile tears had no effect on him; they were water off a duck's back.

The next time I saw Vincent Hale he said the situation was getting serious. He checked the definition of "cake" in the latest edition of the *Oxford English Dictionary*. Although it was still defined as a small, flattish lump of dough, its primary definition was of something containing fruits, spices, etc., so the definition was now somewhat ambiguous. Vincent said, 'You need a solicitor with the resources to take on a case like this,' and on asking him to find me such a solicitor, he phoned me the following week to say he had arranged an appointment for me with Barry Warne of Irwin Mitchell Solicitors.

I went to see Barry. He had studied the papers and said we needed either a precedent or to drag it out for as long as possible. Having applied to the court to lodge an appeal, I had the protection of the court. Further, the case was adjourned so I was able to continue trading for some considerable time. Throughout all this I established a good relationship with Barry Warne and always had

100 per cent confidence in him. At one meeting, to review how the case was going, he said to me, 'For me, this is a crusade against the council. I like nothing better.' (He liked high-profile cases.)

For the next year or so I wrote to bodies all over the country – bakeries, flour millers, universities and others, without success. No-one could precisely define the word "breadcake" and whilst they couldn't help, everyone wished me good luck. I went to see councillors from every party about the market situation. Councillor Alan Billings (Deputy Leader of Sheffield City Council) made representations at the town hall, but no-one seemed to have either the power or the inclination to override Malcolm Prince. Alan Billings said he had made his views known but that his powers were limited. (This, from the Deputy Leader of the Council.) I wrote to every councillor, eighty-two of them, giving them the full history, and all this time the council was still not accepting rent from us. Malcolm Prince ensured this and I am certain he believed we would very quickly finish up in debt, as others had done. We were determined that this wasn't going to happen to us and Joan went to National Provincial Building Society and opened an account. Every week she went across on Monday morning and paid in £300. This more than covered the rent, etc. and made provision for paying the legal costs if it went to the High Court in London and we lost. I also paid our legal fees at Irwin Mitchell as they accrued. At one point we had over £90,000 in the building society, when interest rates were sky-high, and one year we earned over £7,000 interest, after tax. (I remarked to Joan that if Malcolm Prince knew this he'd go mad.) There was a point where we were going to buy Peter Granelli's stall. He wanted £90,000. But Malcolm Prince told Peter the sale wouldn't be allowed to go through. Later on, when we wanted to buy another stall in Castle Market, we bought it in Joan's name only. This way, Malcolm Prince couldn't stop it.

When Joan and I decided to open a Scoop & Save business in Castle Market in 1989 (in Joan's name), we acquired the lease for three units from the receivers who were winding up a business that had been part of Hardy's Bakeries Ltd. and was run by Mrs Hardy. When she first got into difficulties a man called Carter got his hands on the units. He was supposed to be going to turn things around for her but he turned out to be conman full of big ideas, and rent not paid, the business went into receivership. He pocketed the money, obtaining stock from suppliers but not paying. (He had opened one of these units as a scoop shop.) He tried to sell these units to me but asked for the money up-front, and Joan told him to get lost. Eventually I purchased them from Hart, Moss & Copley & Co., accountants. Mr Carter then approached me and I purchased a large amount of stock from him which was in storage. I went to look at it and agreed to buy, making sure that the company storing it knew that it now belonged to me. When I went to collect it, whilst we were loading it, one of the warehouse staff came to me and pointed out another load belonging to Carter. I had never seen it before but I took it, saying, 'Well, you know I've paid Carter, so it belongs to me now,' and loaded it onto my van. Very shortly after, Joan said, 'That man Carter's phoned asking if we want to buy some more stock. I've told him we have enough.' I said, 'He'll have a shock when he finds it's gone.' It was a case of the biter bit. Some months later he was arrested and charged with fraud, and he was sent to prison.

The Scoop & Save was a success from opening. Also, there was a gradual change from being the only one doing battle to people beginning to agree with what I said about Malcolm Prince. (I had repeatedly told any councillor I spoke to of the way Prince treated people.) Further, Prince had tried to prevent me becoming a member of the Market Traders' Committee. He wrote to the chairman, saying that he would refuse to recognize me on the committee or to speak to me. It made no difference, I was voted on. By now, it had become a battle of wills and this went on for six years. (Incidentally, at this time he was the highest paid market superintendent in the country.)

One morning in January 1992 the chairwoman of the Traders' Committee came to see me. She asked if I had heard about Malcolm Price. I hadn't and said, 'What about him?' She said, 'He's leavin', he's been told to take early retirement. Officially it's family health problems but everyone's had enough of him, includin' the council.' I couldn't believe it. Finally! I went up to Central Library to read the minutes of the council meeting and found that he was told he could leave immediately but he'd insisted on serving until the last day of his notice. Well, when that day came, I stood on the bottom loading bay where he parked, making sure he could see me. I watched him carry his personal effects down from his office and load them into his car. He had to make three journeys and when he'd finished and got into his car, I made sure he could see me in his driving mirror as he left the car park.

About two months later, I was in the market on a Thursday morning when Joan came in looking for me. She said Jack Christopher, the Assistant Market Superintendent, had phoned and wanted to see us in his office at 12 o'clock. He was now Acting

Manager. When we went up he was waiting and we shook hands and exchanged first names. (Jack was a completely different character to Malcolm Prince and we never had any quarrel with him.) He said, 'Derek, Joan, I've been given full authority to reach a settlement with you regarding everything that's happened, on the understanding you don't claim costs.' When I started to speak about breadcakes, he said, 'I think we should start with a new user clause. What do you want in it?' I asked for everything I could think of, wishing I'd known this was coming so I could think of as many items as possible. There was no argument. He also said it was on the basis we paid the back rent. Would that be a problem? I told him it was not insurmountable if we could settle everything else and there was no "little black book" somewhere with my name in it. He said, 'Derek, you have my personal word that there isn't, there's nothing like that at all.' Then I asked how much the back rent came to and he told me it was being worked out. Very soon I got a letter telling me the figure was £69,000. I paid £35,000 and the balance in two installments over two months – I didn't want to make it look easy. People have said to me since that I should have said I was sorry, I'd made very little provision for it and I only had half. But I must have had at least £20,000 interest on the building society account so I didn't mind and my good name was intact, which was the most important thing.

CHAPTER 21

QUIDS IN

Going back to the 1970s and 80s, I had been stone cleaning for quite some time but work had dropped off and things were quiet. I had an Austin J U 250 van which, though I had worked it hard, had never let me down, but it developed a problem with the prop shaft which gradually got worse. I knew I needed to replace the prop shaft and I could have got a second-hand one for a fiver, but I didn't have a fiver, so I had to drive slowly and not carry much weight. I am not proud of myself for what I did, but things were really bad: as I was going around, I was keeping my eyes open for a similar van parked up somewhere. I saw exactly the same model in the car park of the Belle Vue pub on Cricket Inn Road. That night I told Joan I had seen this van and what I intended to do. She tried all kinds of ways to talk me out of it but couldn't. Finally she said, 'In that case, you're not going by yourself, I'm going with you, even if it's only to keep watch.' So we waited until about 9 p.m. then drove to the Belle Vue. I parked close to this van, slipped underneath it, and two minutes later the prop shaft was off and in my van. (I had to drive slowly because the one that was on my van knocked loudly.) We got back to Brinsworth Street and fifteen minutes later, and working in the dark, it was on my van. A long time after, I got to know who the owner was when he got five years inside for attempted murder. I'm glad he never got to know who'd had his prop shaft.

By 1979 the council had started demolishing all the houses

around Brinsworth Street and as people were being re-housed, rows and rows of empty houses were boarded up. As soon as a house became vacant thieves would strip it of all the slates, lead, scrap, sometimes within minutes. When the top house in Brinsworth Street was vacated, the vultures moved in, but someone must have seen them and called the police, who came and arrested two men. These men had parked their van away from the house they were stripping and it was full of lead, etc. The police came to our door and asked Joan if she would keep an eye on the van. A while later, they came knocking at our door again. Had we seen anyone drive the van away? Apparently, there were three men, not two, stripping the house and the police had missed the third, so as soon as the police had gone, he came out of hiding and drove the van away with the evidence inside!

The house next to ours was now vacant as Zena and Mohammed had moved to Page Hall. One night, as we were sat in the front room, there was a loud crash outside. We looked out of the window to see a cloud of dust and went out to have a look around. In next door's front garden there was what, at first, I took to be a rolled up carpet but on looking closer, it turned out to be rolled up lead. It was obvious it had come off the top of the bay window of the house. I looked up and down the street. There was a man stood further up and one near the bottom, and they were watching me. I still had the Ford Corsair, so I rolled up the lead as tightly as I could and got my stepson, who was staying with us, to help me. I opened the car boot and we lifted the lead in, which must have been a couple hundredweight, and all this time, these two blokes were watching. I weighed it in the next day.

In 1980 the council exercised their right of compulsory purchase. (Ours was the last house still occupied in Brinsworth Street.) I had asked the council if they would give us a modernization grant and let us stay there. The council official said that once the houses around us were down, we wouldn't want to stay there. When the housing officer came to discuss our moving, she got off to a bad start with Joan by addressing her as the "cohabitee". With her back up, Joan said, sarcastically, 'What's one of those? As far as you're concerned, I am Mrs Naylor and you will address me as such.' Also, we had three dogs: the two Alsatians and a miniature dachshund, and the woman told us we couldn't take three, only one. To this, Joan said, 'So, am I supposed to say to my dogs "You can't go, and you can't go, so you'll have to be put to sleep"? No, thank you. It's you that wants us out, we don't want to go. If we don't take all three dogs, we don't go.'

We started looking around for where we would prefer to be rehoused, and a while later I learned of some new houses that were being built at Spinkhill, just off Prince of Wales Road, so we went to have a look at them. There was a cul-de-sac with about sixteen new houses and a path leading to Bowden Wood. It was Carr Vale View. Joan went to the housing department and asked to have the house at the bottom, on the left-hand side, because we didn't want our dogs to be a nuisance to anyone (although by this time one of the Alsatians had died of old age) and my ice-cream van would be out of the way. At the housing department, they were shocked and told Joan 'You can't pick where you want to go!' meaning, you have what we give you. Joan's reply was much the same as before: 'In that case, we won't be moving. It's you that wants us out, we will stay where we are, thank you!' Joan haunted the housing department and when they were finished, she got the house she wanted.

We moved from Brinsworth Street to Carr Vale View in April 1980. On the day of moving Joan saw to everything at the new house, whilst I saw to our old house. I was determined that the scavengers wouldn't move in the minute we moved out and so, with my dad's help, I set-to stripping the house of everything of value – lead, copper, fireplaces, etc. and an old Yorkshire range. I did the same to Zena's house, next door. I got to the scrap yard just minutes before they closed and weighed in for nearly £70, and when I went home to our new house, Joan had everything in place.

Within three weeks of moving into the house in Carr Vale View, we got a letter from the housing department saying they'd had a complaint about my ice-cream van. I wrote back explaining that I didn't sell ice cream from the house and that I was just like any other self-employed persons such as taxi drivers who kept their vehicles at home, and I mentioned that the new Prime Minister, Margaret Thatcher, was encouraging people to start their own businesses. I also said that I'd done my garden, was parking my van only outside my own house, and I wanted to become a good tenant, but, at the end of the day, I had to earn a living. I didn't hear anything further but, in time, we learned that it was our next door neighbour who had written the letter and that he'd also written complaining about almost everyone in the street.(Eventually everyone was complaining about him.) We were told the council gave him a formal warning about his behaviour, so when he reported us to the RSPCA, saying that our dogs were not being looked after properly, I put a huge board outside our house telling everyone what he had been doing. That shut him up, for a time.

Three years to the day, in 1983, we exercised our right to buy 17 Carr Vale View for £13,500. For this we needed a mortgage and Tim Hale, the son of my solicitor, offered to get me one with Leeds Permanent Building Society but my Nat West bank manager said he could arrange one and I went with him. However, a couple of weeks later he said there was a problem: I wanted £13,500 and the bank's minimum figure was £15,000. I should have said okay, I'll borrow £15,000 but I didn't. The bank manager said, 'Not to worry, Derek, I'll do it for you anyway, it's all the same difference.' Well, almost five years later, checking my bank statements I found that I was paying a higher rate of interest: instead of paying an ordinary mortgage rate, I was paying a business rate. I complained. Their attitude was, "tough shit". I said I wanted the extra money I had paid, that they should pay it back. It went on, them raising all kinds of objections and putting obstacles in my way until finally saying, okay, you calculate how much you say we owe you. It took me months because the interest rates had gone up and down so many times and bank rates and building society rates were never the same. I went to Vincent Hale and he took it up with the bank (and, of course, his charges were increasing). Finally, Nat West offered me an ex gratia settlement of £500 which I reluctantly accepted. It just paid my legal fees. Then I moved my mortgage to Abbey National and my business account to Yorkshire Bank but I left my personal account with Nat West.

My mortgage payment to Abbey National was £134 per month by direct debit. Almost a year later I realised that Nat West were making two (unconnected) payments of £134 per month to Abbey

187

National. I thought to myself, right, you carry on, I'm not going to tell you, you can find out for yourselves. My mortgage was going down and down and so was the interest on it. I thought they'd soon realise their mistake but they didn't and this went on for years. Eventually I received a letter from a firm of London based solicitors acting for Nat West. They had become aware of the mistake at the end of 1995 because the bank had another client with the same name as mine who had been living in South Africa and had recently moved back the UK. On checking his financial affairs, he had started asking questions. Now I was being asked to repay the extra money, nearly £14,000, and the bank had to reimburse the other D. Naylor plus interest and compensation. I wrote saying this was a big shock to me, that I hadn't realised what had been happening and that I didn't have the means to repay anything. I pointed out that it was their mistake and, anyway, they couldn't claim anything going back more than six years. Letters went back and forth and theirs were always so polite and understanding. I thought to myself, they're not sure what sort of case they've got. I discussed it with Steve Dunwell, the manager at Yorkshire Bank. (We got on great, he wasn't your usual manager.) His advice was, and these are his exact words, 'Derek, tell 'em to fuck off. Their mistake, they won't tek it to court. They won't want the bad publicity.' He was adamant that I should say get lost or words to that effect but I wasn't so sure. I knew there was a difference: once I knew of their mistake, I should have informed them. I hadn't. I'd had a good run for my money.

I went to see the Nat West manager (at High Street branch) a couple of times, making sure I was shabbily dressed and unshaven, my daughter with me for support because I was unsteady on my feet. Whilst appearing a bit vague, I asked him to put the matter to one side until after Christmas. He was very understanding and said he would. A couple of months later, the bank's solicitors wrote to me again. I felt that if it went to court I could lose and might have to pay back the full amount plus costs, so I made them an offer of £6,000 for full and final settlement. They accepted without hesitation and said that if it would help I could pay it back over a given period, which I did. I also thought that perhaps Steve Dunwell had been right after all, but I'd had the last laugh, the bastards.

CHAPTER 22

REMEMBERING AUNT NELL

When I left my first wife, Mary, and went with Joan, my mother's attitude towards Mary changed. Suddenly, after all those years when she never had a good word to say about her, Mary now could do no wrong; she never stopped singing her praises and even persuaded Mary to move nearer to her. Mary had remarried and I met her new husband. He was a nice man. When my mother told me she had also met him, she went on to tell me that he looked a lot younger than me. That really was below the belt.

I continued going to see my mother and father but it wasn't long before my mother did the same thing to Joan that she had initially done to Mary, the cold treatment. My mother used to come to the market every Saturday when I was serving at the front of the stall. I would see her walking up the aisle towards me and I'd will her to look at me but she never did. Instead, she would turn her head sideways until she'd gone past and even though I sold Nuttall's Mintoes, which she loved, not once did she come to my stall. She would buy them elsewhere. So my mother made it clear she that didn't like Joan and she wasn't welcome, but Joan was a different character to Mary and said she wasn't going to lose any sleep over my mother, though it did hurt me. (The relationship between my mam, my dad and me was complicated, even after I had grown up and had my own family. And though my parents had a set of kids that thought the world of them they never realised it.) But despite everything, I continued going to see her almost every week until she died.

I heard that my dad wasn't very well. By now he was 72 years old. It was a Saturday morning and I went to see him. He was sitting in his chair when he suddenly grimaced, saying, 'Fuckin' 'ell,' whilst holding his side for a few seconds. I asked what was wrong. 'It's tha' fuckin' pain again,' he said. I spoke to my mother and she said he'd been to see the doctor, who told him it was pleurisy. It was early Saturday morning so I went back to the market where I told Joan there was something wrong with my dad. I then phoned my mother and asked her to make an appointment with the doctor for Monday morning, saying I'd go with him, which she did. Meanwhile, I went to see Rosita Granelli whose mother-in-law had recently seen a doctor privately, and I asked Rosita for the name of this doctor. On the Monday morning I went with my dad to see his GP, a Dr Nightingale, at Manor Top, and told her my father was having severe pain. She said, 'Oh, well, I'll give him something else.' I said no, I wanted him to see a specialist and I gave her the name. She didn't like this very much but said in that case he might as well see the doctor he'd seen about two years before at the Hallamshire who would have his notes. I said okay and she told me there would be a letter of introduction ready for picking up anytime after 12 o'clock on the Wednesday. On my way back to my parents' house I thought to myself, that's a long time to wait for a letter of perhaps four or five lines. So I phoned the GP and said I wanted it sooner than Wednesday. I got it that day and took it up to Dr Derek Cullen and I received a phone call in the afternoon about an appointment.

Within a few days of my dad having x-rays and various tests

done, the consultant phoned at around 8 p.m. saying it was as he feared: my father had cancer of the stomach. I arranged to see Dr Cullen the next day when he would explain more fully what he'd found and what we should do. I was told my dad's only chance was surgery but my dad had always said that no-one was going to carve him up, and I added that he was of a very nervous disposition. The doctor's reply was, 'In that case, nature will take its course', he went on, 'but forget all you hear about cancer patients dying in agony. He will come onto my ward at the Hallamshire, and he will be my patient, and there will be no pain.' This would be towards the end of the week and I asked Dr Cullen to find a good surgeon.

I called a meeting of my brothers and sisters for the Sunday, at my house, to tell them of my father's illness and what I thought needed to be done: an operation, done privately. (Joan and I had discussed it beforehand and we were both agreed.) I asked my siblings to contribute £300 each and Joan and I would pay the rest. They all agreed and so my father was admitted to Claremont Hospital on the Tuesday or Wednesday and the operation was the following day. On the Friday I received a phone call at work, around 9.30 a.m. It was from the hospital to say that my father's condition had deteriorated overnight and that we should go immediately. Joan told me to get off, that she would see to everything at work. I dashed down to Stones Brewery where my brother Lawrence was working and then, quick as we could, up to the hospital. Dr Cullen and Mr Robertson the surgeon were both there and had been since 4 a.m. Dr Cullen said my father had been given every drug possible and there was nothing more they could do. Apparently he'd had a mild stroke and cardiac arrest had occurred. A sister was just coming out of my father's room, so I approached her and said I wanted my father to have a priest. She told me, 'Your father had the last sacraments at 6 o'clock this morning, and now he is going home to God.' As my mother didn't yet know and the sister said she thought she should be there, we went to my sister Gloria's house, where my mother was staying, to tell her and take her back to the hospital.

To everyone's amazement he pulled through and was back home two weeks later. After a few days I called up to see how he was. My mother told me he'd gone up to see one of the nurses who had looked after him, having already visited the other nurse. They had looked after him really well in hospital, and he had bought each of them a gold watch to say thank you. I thought to myself, and we've been struggling to pay the fucking hospital bills! But neither of my parents ever asked how his operation had been arranged or paid for. So I was paying the bills one at a time – the room, tests, x-rays, drugs, surgeon, etc., and the last bill I paid was for the x-rays. I took the cheque up to Claremont, to a Mr Grainger, consultant radiologist, and I apologised for being late paying. He asked after my father. When I said he was great and was out helping my brother on a job (and by this time he was enjoying his usual pint of beer), Mr Grainger said he was very surprised to hear that he was doing so well and admitted that he had been hesitant about asking because he expected me to tell him that my father had died. When I paid Dr Cullen's bill, I asked him what my father's chances of coming through a major operation had been. 'Just 5 per cent,' he said. My father went on to live another nine and a half years.

Reflecting on things, I remembered the days of Aunt Nell, the old lady who had been like a second mother and used to come round to our house of an evening. As me and my brothers and sisters grew older my mother didn't need her so much. When we saw her coming up the street it would be to ask if my mother wanted anything from town or the market. My mother would lock the door and tell us to keep quiet and Aunt Nell would be knocking on the door and saying, 'Is tha there, Lily?' Eventually she would go away and finally she stopped coming.

My wife Mary was a very good knitter and she made many things for me and the children. She knitted me a really good sweater in salmon pink chunky wool which I was wearing one Sunday when I went to see my mother. As I was walking down Southend Road Aunt Nell was walking up. She was, by now, very elderly and her eyesight was extremely poor so she didn't recognise me and I had to stop her. When she realised it was me she exclaimed, 'Oh, it's our Derek!' She was wearing her pixie hood, and her coat was wrapped around her tightly, with her hands inside it. She looked so cold I took off my sweater and made her put it on.

I never saw Aunt Nell again. I think she would have ended her days in the Little Sisters of the Poor, a Catholic refuge in East Road, opposite Olive Grove. It was run by nuns to help poor elderly people of the parish who were sick or frail and who had nowhere else to go and she used to speak of them and the good they did. When I got to my mother's, I told her I had seen Aunt Nell and that I'd given her my sweater because she was so cold. She told me I shouldn't have done, that she'd just sell it. I said, 'If she does, she does.'

Some year later, when I was crossing the road after coming out of the market, I saw an old woman coming towards me. She was so thin and looked so poor I was reminded of Aunt Nell. I turned around and went after her. I had a five-pound note in my pocket so I stopped her and pushed it into her hand, saying, 'I think you've just dropped this, love,' and then hurried away before she could look to see what it was or say anything. (I've known what it's like not to have two halfpennies to rub together and I've never forgotten what it's like so, in my own way, I try to give something back, without anyone knowing my reasons.)

Around the same time, there was a public appeal to raise money for famine relief in Eritrea. A woman was standing outside the market collecting and she had a big poster depicting a starving woman and baby. I asked if she would give me the poster when she had finished collecting and I put it up on my stall along with a sweet jar with a slot in the top. I did the same at Hillsborough and we collected about £400. I arranged for my bank to count it and send off a cheque. When the Falklands War started I collected for that, too. I don't remember how much it came to but it was mentioned in *The Star* and I took a cheque up to the fund that was opened at the town hall. I also donated to David Blunkett's appeal to raise money for a reward for information leading to the capture of the person or persons who had blinded a horse that was grazing in a field. Many months later he returned my cheque with a very kind letter saying, unfortunately, that whoever was responsible for the gross act hadn't been caught.

CHAPTER 23

GREAT HAPPINESS; GREAT SORROW

Joan and I had been together for ten years. I had asked her to marry me more than once and she always said the same thing – that as far as she was concerned we were married and she couldn't feel more married. But this time, instead of leaving it at that, I went to the register office and gave seven days' notice to marry by special licence and completed all the paperwork. That done, I went back to the market and took Joan off the stall to ask her if she had made any plans for the following Thursday. She said no and asked why. 'Because we're getting married.' She said, only, 'Are we?' I assured her that we were, indeed, and her face lit up; she was delighted.

One of those invited to our wedding was our bank manager, Mike Higginbottom. He had quite a sense of humour. I recall him telling me, after he'd retired, that he and his wife Peggy were having breakfast one morning when Peggy said, 'Mike, I need your advice as I'm thinking of changing my will.' He asked how much they were talking about and when Peggy told him, he saw that it was a lot of money and it set him thinking. The following morning he said to her, 'What about us getting married?' which Peggy had been wanting for a long time. He told me, after they had made the arrangements, 'I've said to Peggy, "Let's forget about you changing your will, okay, love?"' In similar humour, when we were having our wedding photos taken, Mike was stood at the back shouting, 'Over here, Derek, Joan, over here!' and I looked to see him waving a huge pair of ladies old-fashioned, interlocking knickers in the air!

So we were married on 16 May 1985. It was a quiet wedding with just a few family and friends, and after the ceremony we went to Tuckwoods restaurant. Our celebration was rounded off by spending four days in Bridlington. We were so happy! (I also bought Joan a Siamese kitten as she loved cats and she had him until he died of old age.)

My mother hadn't been on speaking terms with us, again, and didn't know about our wedding. I'm sure that if she had, she would have turned up and created a scene because she really had her knife into Joan. When I went up a few days after and told her about our marriage, she didn't say a word, nothing. The following year I was at my mother's when she told me, only as I was leaving, that my brother Terrence was in hospital and had undergone a major operation for cancer of the oesophagus. Apparently he had been ill for some time and I just couldn't understand why she had kept it from me; it was twelve days after his operation and I had only just been told! And I saw my mother often. I hadn't seen Terrence for some while because of a silly argument between us, and I went home and wrote him a letter telling him I'd only just learned of his illness. I asked if we could put everything behind us and asked for his forgiveness, and could I see him. When I took the letter to the hospital (Beechwood), they said he had been discharged that morning. I went to his home but he'd just gone out, so I gave the letter to his son. A few days later he came to the market to see me. We had made up. From then on I made sure we saw a lot of one another.

Terrence worked for Bass Charrington and they were brilliant. His treatment and care at the private hospital were paid for through their medical scheme, and he remained on full pay throughout his illness and convalescence. When he wanted to go back to work, several months later, they tried to dissuade him and said he would remain on full pay indefinitely but Terrence insisted on going back. However, a few months in he had to admit that he couldn't do his job anymore and asked for redundancy. They could have denied him redundancy pay but, as I said, they were decent employers and gave it him. One of the bosses asked him what he planned to do. Terrence didn't know. The boss told him they had a nice little pub coming vacant and though it wasn't fashionable, it would give him a nice living if he wanted it. Even though my brother was virtually teetotal he said yes.

The pub was The Albert in Worksop Road. Terrence set out to make a few alterations, spending about £12,000, and apart from being alright for money, he loved it. My younger sister, Gloria, and her husband were experienced in the pub trade and were very supportive of my brother and his wife. However, just a few months after taking over he fell very ill again. The cancer had come back. My sister and her husband looked after the pub for him, and as he was still covered by Bass Charrington's medical scheme, I took him to the hospital to see the surgeon who had operated on him the first time.

Seeing the surgeon, Mr J.A.R Smith, was heartbreaking. Terrence asked him about a second operation and Mr Smith explained that an operation can only be done once. My brother asked what his options were, finally saying to Mr Smith, 'You're sayin' there's nothin' further you can do?' The answer was chilling. When Terrence asked Mr Smith how long he'd got left he told us six to nine months. The only thing that could be done was for a peg (a tube) to be fitted for him to be fed directly into his stomach. So this was done.

I don't know where my brother summoned the courage from, but he put all his affairs in order and then he bought all his family Christmas presents for when he'd gone. He'd transferred the pub licence to his wife, and my sister and her husband continued to run it. Terrence died on 28 October 1988 aged 52.

At this point, I have to pay tribute to my sister Gloria and to her husband Michael for the way they supported and helped my brother Terrence and his family. They were brilliant. Thank you.

When Joan and I were well established in the market, my mother's eldest sister, Hilda, used to come to the market regularly. Joan was still persona non grata as far as my mother was concerned, but Hilda always made a point of coming to our stall to have a chat with her. She told us that she was having a family party to celebrate her diamond wedding anniversary, 'An' you are invited.' I said I didn't think we'd be able to make it and she said, 'Ah know all about your mother, and you are comin'.' Joan and I decided we would go but would leave early. The party was at a pub near the junction of Wood Street and Langsett Road and we got there around 9 p.m. My mother was sat down near the stage with all her sisters, laughing and joking, and my dad was sat at a table on his own so we sat down with him. Clearly, he'd had a drink but he wasn't drunk. We asked him how he was doing and then he said to me, 'Thi mother's down there, go an' talk to 'er.' I told him, 'In a bit,' but he said it again and again, getting louder and more insistent. I repeated myself, but then he said, 'Wha's tha ever done for me? Tha's never fuckin' done owt for me!' I didn't reply, I just thought to myself, Dad, if only you knew. Joan said to me, 'Come on love, let's go.' And so we left. I still feel so sad whenever I think about that night and I go quiet, but it never stopped me loving him.

Towards the end of my father's life he became delicate and frail and in many ways it was his spirit that kept him going. My mother didn't go out very much as she was limited in what she could do because of arthritis, and my sister Gloria did a great deal for my parents. But my dad still liked to go down town when he could and he'd do my mother a bit of shopping. He used to enjoy going round the market but he seldom stopped at our stall to say hello, he'd usually walk straight past. One day when I got back to the market after being out buying stock, Joan told me that my dad had been in the market and as he walked past our stall, one of the younger members of staff went to Joan and told her that he looked very ill. Joan went after him and brought him back, sitting him down at The Soda Fountain snack bar opposite us. She asked her friend Jackie, the owner, to look after him whilst she went to get her car out of the car park to take him home. When they got there, she helped him up the steps and knocked on the door. My mother helped him into the house as Joan explained that she'd brought him home because he'd become ill whilst in the market, but my mother shut the door, leaving Joan stood on the step. She never spoke one word to my wife. That was my mother.

Two years later my dad died. Shortly before, I had called in to see him and my mother on a Saturday afternoon. He was quite fragile and didn't say very much, while my mother was restless. My younger sister came in and I left soon after. Unusually, my dad came to the door with me but he didn't say anything. I got into my car and reversed down the street and as I did so he waved to me. I waved back but really I felt I wanted to stop the car and go back to him; he had stayed on the step, just watching me go, and for that second I wanted to go back and put my arms around him and say, 'I love you, Dad.' But I knew he'd feel embarrassed and I didn't do it. The following week I was told he was in the Northern General Hospital. I went up to see him, first going to speak with his doctor. I asked if I could visit out of hours, saying that it was difficult for me to get there at the usual visiting times. He told me, 'Mr Naylor, you can visit your father at any time.' When I saw my dad, he said he had a bad headache, so I went to ask the nurse for something to help and she gave me a couple of tablets. I put my arms around him, helping him to sit up to take the pills. It was the first time in my life I had ever put my arms around him.

The next night I visited him with Joan. Yet again, my mother and sister were being cold and distant from me, and we sat outside until the other visitors had left and then I went to him for a couple of minutes. The following day was Sunday and I had said to Joan that I would go up early, before anyone else, but I know that I was dilatory. And then, around midday, my brother-in-law Harry phoned to say, 'Derek, we've just 'ad a telephone call from the 'ospital. Your dad has just died.' We were told that the previous day my father had gone to the other three men on the ward to shake their hands. And If I hadn't been so dozy I might have been with him instead of him dying alone. He died in November 1990 at the age of 81.

In his last years he was still getting out and about and always enjoyed a pint (sometimes getting a little drunk). I was calling in to see them and he would come and see me and, overall, he enjoyed the last years of his life. And while there is much more to this part of my life, it is too personal and painful for me to talk about, so I'm sure my readers will forgive me for keeping it private.

My brother Lawrence and I decided that my father wouldn't have a cheap funeral and we would see to the invoice. Two to three weeks after, I asked my brother about the invoice and he said, 'Derek, it's paid, my mother 'as insisted on payin' it 'erself. It were the last thing she could do for 'im an' she's got a nice little nest egg.' She had always believed in insurance, 6d and 1/- policies, some of which she had for almost fifty years. But when my father died, in a sense her life ended; she missed him so much. (She had a large photo of him and she said she always kissed it goodnight before going to bed.) She died at home two years later on Christmas Day 1992.

When my father died, my mother was 79 years old and had severe osteoarthritis, as well as asthma. I was still calling in every week, timing my visits so that there was no-one else at the house when I called, just me and her. My sister Gloria used to go up and would often have my mother to stay with them but my brother Lawrence was the one who called every evening. He'd go straight from work and she used to cook him a hot tea and have hers with him. Whilst this ensured that she looked after herself and ate regularly, it also meant that my brother would have to eat another hot tea when he got home and he kept this up for two years.

In the last year of her life my birthday fell on a Sunday. That day, around mid-afternoon, there was a knock at the door and my brother walked in with my mother. It was such a surprise I couldn't speak. Lawrence said, 'Derek, ah've brought my mother over, she wanted to see tha.' I put my arms around her, holding her tight. We were both in tears. And I am as I write this. Lawrence then told me, 'She's brought thee a birthday present.' It was the first in all my life and was a gold St Christopher medal and chain. I turned around so she could put it round my neck. Again, we were both in tears. I held her. She was so small and defenceless. I said to her, 'Mam, why don't you come and see me more often?' Her reply was the plain and simple truth: 'Ah'd love to but ah daren't, ah'm too frightened.' I knew what she meant. We talked for a while, our arms around one another. After a short while she said to Lawrence, 'Tek me 'ome now.' I made sure that I called to see her every week at a time when she'd be alone in the house.

Christmas Eve came. I called in on my mother that afternoon and asked her what she was doing that night. She told me Lawrence was going to pick her up and take her, with them, to the little club "Libs" in Attercliffe. I said I would see her on Christmas Day. That morning, at about 10.30, I was sat having a pot of tea with Joan. We'd both worked right to the end of Christmas Eve and were shattered. Startling us, the phone rang. It was my brother. He said, 'Derek, ah'm at my mother's. She's collapsed. She managed to get downstairs to tek bolt off door so I could get int' house. She's collapsed at bottom of stairs. Ah've got 'er int' front room an' ah'm tryin' t' give 'er the kiss o' life. Phone the ambulance an' police, ah'm tryin' to get 'er to breathe but, Derek, ah think she's died!' I was out of the house and over there within minutes. The ambulance and the police had just arrived, then my sisters. Lawrence was inconsolable, blaming himself. He said he had driven at 90 m.p.h to get to her, but too late. He told me that when he was taking her home on Christmas Eve, she told him her nebuliser wasn't working and he said he would see to it the next day. He was saying, 'Ah should 'ave gone in an' done it there and then.' We both new that as I lived the nearest I

203

might have got there perhaps a few minutes earlier than him. But would it have made any difference? I don't know. What we did know was that it would have caused friction in certain quarters. My mother also knew this and perhaps that's why she didn't call me. No-one will ever know.

My mother was buried in City Road Cemetery, alongside my dad. I was the eldest in the family, and as the eldest son, I should have taken charge of her funeral and her estate but, again, this wouldn't have gone down very well. So I asked Lawrence to take charge, with Gloria, and settle her affairs, just keeping me informed, which he did. And even though her house stayed in the family for quite some time after her death, I never went into that house again.

My sisters arranged a buffet at the Trades & Labour Club in Duke Street for after the funeral. Me and Joan, my daughters and two of my mother's sisters were sat near the door; my sisters and other family members were sat near the bar. After a while, a cousin named Margaret, who I'd not seen for over thirty years, was getting ready to leave. When she saw us she came over and talked with my two aunts. It soon became clear that not only was she was talking about me, she was being very offensive. I finally told her I thought she should leave and got her to the door. I then sat down again, not noticing that Joan wasn't there. Minutes later she came and sat beside me and when I asked her where she'd been, she said, 'I've been out to that Margaret. You don't think I was going to let her get away with what she said about you, do you? I followed her out and told her, "No-one speaks about my husband like you've just done." Bang. Derek, I've only hit her once, but I've nearly knocked her head off her fucking shoulders.' That was just like my wife: I always knew she would go through fire and water for me.

My father with his accordion, my mother and two of
my parents' granddaughters at Southend Place

CHAPTER 24

A NEW YEAR; A NEW LEASE OF LIFE

So I had lost my brother Terrence to cancer in 1988, my dad to cancer in 1990 and my mother to asthma and heart attack in 1992. I still really miss my brother and my dad, and I am genuinely surprised at how much I miss my mother. But life goes on and by now I had decided to sell the Hillsborough business and spend more time on leisurely pursuits, so in early 1994 my wife and I decided to buy a caravan, a good static one. It was summer, and we and two friends went for a weekend away in Scarborough to look around caravan parks. As we had no success, we thought we'd have a weekend in Bridlington a fortnight on, just the two of us. On the Friday, the day before our trip, I drove my 20-foot Ford Cargo van, with a taillift, to Hancocks Ltd., a confectionary wholesaler, where I bought a pallet of coffee, two pallets of Cadbury chocolate bars plus a mixed pallet and some other items. I spent a lot of money. My van was parked on the loading bay at Castle Market, the warehouse being on the lower ground floor, and the last thing I did was to tell my stepson Mark that I wanted it unloading. There wasn't any room in the warehouse, as it was, so he'd have to rearrange things and then unload the van. Joan and I went to Bridlington early the next morning.

Well, we found a top of the range, 36 x 12 ft luxury caravan, only ten months old. The owner wanted £13,500. We were delighted but when we got back home on the Monday evening, Joan sensed straight away that something wasn't right, and it wasn't long before her son came to tell us that whilst we were away, the van had been stolen off the loading bay and the chocolate, the coffee and everything else on it had gone. After I had recovered enough to ask if the police had been informed, he said yes, they were treating it as a stolen vehicle. I said, 'I'm not bothered about the van, that's insured. It's the stock, £9,000 worth, and that's not!' I reminded him that I'd told him to unload it and he hadn't done so. His only response was that I should have insisted that he unload it. I felt sick. Furthermore, I had to go to the police three times before they would treat it seriously as stolen goods and not just vehicle theft. Four days later they found the empty van at Royston, near Barnsley. Significantly, it had been unloaded using a forklift truck (the roller shutter back having been ripped off). I got the van repaired but never recovered any stock, though I had my own strong suspicions as to what had really happened.

My wife asked if this meant we wouldn't be having the caravan. I told her we could still have it and I made an offer of £12,500. A friend with a caravan nearby had looked at it and said it was a bargain so it would soon go. I was saying to Joan that he'd take my offer, just wait a couple of days but she phoned the caravan salesman, telling him, 'Take no notice of my husband, we'll have it.' She told me this and I said okay and we got the caravan; however, every time we planned to go there for the weekend her son Mark would find some way of thwarting our plans. He was acting manager at Punch Stores and he'd say something like he would be short of staff if his mother was absent, or he was already short-staffed because of holidays, any excuse. Many times I felt sick to death of him and just wanted rid of him but Joan would always ask me to give him another chance, saying, 'Derek, love, I'll talk to him. He's got a mortgage to pay,' etc., etc., and I always did give him another chance; she was his mother, and she was an equal partner in the business. And she knew how much I loved her. So, sadly, we never got to use the caravan much and I ended up selling it five years later.

By November 1995 it became clear that Joan was run down and unwell. I asked her if she would go to Claremont Hospital for a Well Woman examination if I arranged it and she agreed. When she came home after the examination, she said the doctor had hurt her and she continued to be in pain for the next two weeks. I phoned the doctor and told him, 'You appear to have triggered something off.' He said, 'I think she should see Mr Smith.' I asked if he meant J.A.R Smith, the surgeon. He said yes and arranged it. However, by the time we went to see Mr Smith she was in such pain he wasn't able to examine her, so he arranged for her to go into Claremont and go into theatre for an examination under sedation. Afterwards, he phoned me. They'd detected a suspicious lump and would I go up that night so he could explain his findings? There, he disclosed that Joan had bowel cancer and he gently told me it would mean having a stoma (an opening) with a pouch, permanently. Since it was very late, I asked him not to say anything to Joan until the next morning.

The week before Christmas we went to Mr Smith's house. It was Thursday night. He took us through the operation, in detail, and when he'd finished, said he could do it the following morning. He was a first-class surgeon and said his fee was £2,000. To my shame, I asked him how much for cash in a brown envelope. He said £1,900. But Joan said she couldn't go in because we were going on holiday after Christmas. He asked when we'd be back. 6 January. 'No', he said, 'but have Christmas Day at home and come in Boxing Day. I'll do it the following morning.'

She was in theatre for five hours, and the care and support she received was excellent. As she was in for New Year's Eve, I ordered a couple of bottles of champagne. The friends we'd planned to go to Israel with after Christmas came up to see her and they left another bottle but since there was no-one else in the hospital, I shared it with the nurses. I stayed until nearly 2 a.m. Joan was worrying about me getting stuck in the snow when going home, but the caretaker told me that if I found myself snowed in he would find me a bed.

Joan came home twelve days later. She had to have radiotherapy for four weeks (which was worse than the operation) and her weight went down to less than 7 stone, but she was determined to beat the illness and within four months she was back at work part time and within eight months she was back to working full time. (She worked until she was 69 years old.)

CHAPTER 25

MY WORLD IS CHANGED

Late one Friday afternoon I was out in my van, having been to Hancocks Cash and Carry on the off-chance they might have something of interest. From there I went to H & H Wholesale further up the road. Though it was dark, as I approached the loading bay I noticed a silver Vauxhall Cavalier parked at the side. I reversed into the loading bay and went into the warehouse, which was in semi-darkness. I walked past the office, on my right, and saw two men about 30 feet in front of me both wearing ski masks. I turned my head to look in through the office window and saw it was empty. When I turned back again, the two men were in front of me, one holding a revolver, the other a machete (and standing as still as if he were on guard at Buckingham Palace). I thought, fucking hell, the revolver might be imitation but I don't think that machete is! The bloke holding the revolver shoved it right under my chin, shouting, 'Where's the safe? Where's the fuckin' safe?' I shouted back, 'I don't fucking know, I'm a fucking customer!' He shouted back at me not to 'fuckin' move' and took a running kick at the office door. As it flew open, he grabbed me and pushed me into the office, shouting, 'Get down, get down.' I knelt down on the floor. He saw the safe but it was huge and must have weighed a ton and he could see he'd have no luck with it, so they went out into the warehouse, leaving me knelt on the floor. I knew they were looking for the manager, Pete Marshall, and I gave them a few seconds before getting to my feet and going to the door. I couldn't see anyone. I flew out of the warehouse, took a running jump off the loading bay and tore across the yard into the unit opposite. As I ran, I heard Pete Marshall shout, 'Derek, 'e's got a gun!' I thought, I know he's got a fucking gun! I hope he can't see me in the dark!

The police and Police Armed Response unit were there in minutes but the two men had already fled the scene. Lots of detectives looked around and took statements. I gave my statement to a policewoman whilst sat in her car and she remarked on how calm I was. As I was walking to my van, the detective in charge called out to me, 'What's your name?' When I told him, he said, 'Oh, yes, I've 'eard about you.' (I've always wondered what he meant by that.) They wouldn't let me drive my van home so the policewoman drove me. Later that night the owner of H & H Wholesale, Pete Hobson, phoned me to ask if I was alright. I thought I might get a bottle or two of whiskey off him but I didn't even get a thank you. The next morning I went to collect my van. There were some customers stood around Pete, listening to him tell about what had happened. One of the customers known as Big Richard, said, 'Ah don't know, ah think ah would 'ave 'ad to 'ave a go.' I thought, bollocks you would!

What these two thugs didn't know, and I found out later, was that Securicor came at about 4 o'clock every afternoon, and so, for all their efforts, the safe would have been empty. They were caught a few months later when someone got their car registration number as they tried to rob a petrol station at Meadowhead.

Joan was doing really and we decided on a holiday in Spain. We also went to Royal Ascot – she loved Ladies' Day – and we made a week of it, as usual, with friends Alec and Jackie, first going to Brighton and then to London for sightseeing and a show. This year it was *Chicago* followed by a marvellous meal and we always stayed at a top hotel.

Not long afterwards, Joan told me that her younger son was getting married and as the couple's plans unfolded it became clear that it was going to cost us. The first thing was that he owed me £2,000. I told him to keep it and put it towards the wedding. I never questioned Joan about money or the cost of anything and her son knew this. Joan would say she'd told them we'd pay for that, then she would tell them we'd pay for this, then that, then something else, but as far as I'm aware, she was never thanked for anything. So he got married on a Sunday at Sheffield Cathedral and it finished with Joan and myself paying for everything, including three weeks' honeymoon at a five star hotel in Cancun, Mexico, and a week in London.

By now I was beginning to think about retirement. There had been much talk and plans made for building a new market but since this had been going on for some years, I had begun to think I wouldn't see it. I talked to Joan about it. She didn't want to think about selling up and retiring but, for once, I was determined and, after all, she loved me very much. As I did her. (If she got home and I was late back from buying, always she would come to the door to greet me with a kiss and if no-one else was there, she'd say, 'Hello, my darling, glad you're home.' The happiest part of my life.) So, decision made, I put the Scoop & Save up for sale in 1999. The business agents quickly found a buyer and then another couple came along with a better offer but it fell through so we went with the first offer. After a lengthy period, the sale went through to a man called Kevin Polky who was a very nice person but had no previous experience of market life. Nevertheless, he said he also wanted to buy Punch Stores and I gave him a good price, with which he was very happy. However, Joan was worried about her son Mark's future. I decided to offer Kevin Polky a reduction in price if he would keep her son on as an employee, which he did, and Punch Stores was sold in October 2000. Joan carried on working there until the Easter of 2001.

For some time I had been having a battle with an insurance company regarding a claim for subsidence damage to our home. It was serious, affecting a large extension which had been built ten years previously. The case had dragged on. At first they wouldn't accept my claim so I employed one of the best surveyors in the country. They then accepted it but said it could be repaired. We refused this and said we wanted demolition and rebuild. Around this time, Joan was becoming unwell again. (We'd enjoyed a good two years, taking holidays in the Lake District and abroad after selling the businesses.) I always worried about her smoking and tried many times to get her to stop. She did try but said to me, 'Derek, love, you've never smoked so you don't know how hard it is to stop.' She'd been smoking since she was 13 and I knew it was a pleasure for her, so I stopped nagging.

I gradually realized that my wife was very ill, and I reached a settlement with the insurance company, a cash agreement, and we would demolish and rebuild, ourselves. I found a good building firm and arranged the demolition. Joan was in hospital by now and I wanted to postpone everything but she said to get on with it whilst she was in hospital, so the demolition work started on 21 April 2004.

Joan was in the Northern General and one of the few people there for us during this time was Joan's niece Nancy. No matter what time of day or night it was she would be there. We saw very little of others in the family. Fortunately, we had good friends in Gerry and Flo Allerston. When they came, which was often, they would bring Joan a little treat and Flo would always bring flowers, which Joan loved, and Gerry would sit talking with Joan and holding her hand. Later, when his daughter got married, his family and friends came from all over the world and Gerry introduced Joan to them all as his very special friend. Another who was there for us at this time was my son Derek. He is a plumber and heating engineer and when our home was being rebuilt, he did all the plumbing and tiling, fitted a new boiler, new kitchen and even more. He didn't just sit there saying how sorry he felt for me, he helped, and while I don't see a great deal of him now, I shall never forget what he did for me when I really needed someone.

2004 was a truly dreadful year. Joan was constantly in and out of hospital and eventually we were told it was terminal lung cancer. Nancy arranged a party for Joan's 72nd birthday and while she came out for the afternoon, she had to be back for 7 p.m. Thankfully, after everyone had gone home, we were able to have the last hour to ourselves. The time came for me to take her back to the hospital, but as I was reversing off the drive, lo and behold, the manhole cover collapsed and the front wheel got wedged in the hole. So I had to use a batten under the front of the car to lift it out, and as ill as Joan was, she got out of the car to help me, reminding me of what she used to say: 'Derek, you could have a Rolls Royce and sooner or later I'd have to push it,' and we had a good chuckle about it.

Early in October the hospital sent for me and Joan. We were told that the chemotherapy hadn't worked and there was nothing more they could do. Joan just said to me, 'Let's go home.' Once, when I said that if only she could have stopped smoking sooner (she had stopped some time before when they said it was cancer), she told me, again, that she didn't want to stop because she enjoyed smoking and had only given it up because she had to. But she was worried about how I would look after myself when she had gone. She re-arranged all my clothes in the wardrobe and put all my shoes (and I had many pairs) back in the correct boxes, writing a description on each box. She showed me how to work the washing machine and which cupboards and drawers contained which items so I knew where everything was, all the whilst telling me 'Don't cry, love.' She never once indulged in self-pity, and even when she was in pain, she would tell me how much she loved me. One evening towards the end of the month, she asked me to sit beside her. She said, 'Derek, I don't want to go into hospital. I want you to look after me.' I made her a solemn promise that I would and told her doctor, Dr Bottomly, he mustn't raise the matter of hospital. (We saw very little of family. It was as if they were afraid.)

On 9 December Doctor Bottomly phoned to ask if he could visit. I said yes. When he came that afternoon, he asked her if she would consider going into hospital 'Just for a few days to give Derek a break.' I was so angry with him. Joan was still mentally very alert and she asked me, 'What do you think I should do?' I reminded her of my promise; if I had said yes to her going into hospital, she would have gone and I would have broken that promise. She agreed to have a Macmillan nurse, and a senior nurse and a doctor came within two hours and helped her upstairs and into bed.

Almost her last words to me were how well I had cared for her and how much she loved me. She died in my arms 36 hours later at 1.25 a.m. on Saturday 11 December 2004. All her family and her best friend, June, were present. When everyone had left, I lay with her for the rest of that night, with my arms around her, and fell fast asleep until daylight. I loved her so much.

I don't know how I got through that first Christmas without her but I did, with the help of my son and daughters. She had some beautiful clothes that I gave to Cancer Research and we also collected £380 for St. Luke's Hospice, which Gerry and I took to them. Gerry also sent a cheque to Cancer Research. Joan always bought the best of everything for me, herself, the family. She also loved springing pleasant surprises on me and among my many special memories is this wonderful weekend:

This particular week she had been very quiet and mysterious. On the Friday evening she was busy ironing and when I went upstairs I saw a suitcase packed. I asked her what was going on but she wouldn't say anything, just smiled and carried on. Finally, she asked me if I knew where Leeds Bradford Airport was. I said yes and asked her why and she announced that we had to be there at 9.30 the following morning but she wouldn't say anything more. I thought, lovely, she must have booked us a holiday in Spain. So on the Saturday we got to the airport to find another two couples there who were also from Sheffield. One of the men I recognized and when I went across to talk to him, Joan piped up, 'Don't tell him anything. He doesn't know!' Then a tall, well-spoken gentleman approached us and after asking our names, said, 'I'm your pilot.' Again, Joan quickly said, 'He doesn't know, so don't tell him!' We followed him out of the airport building and across the grass to a small twin engine plane. Our cases were put into the luggage compartment, and when we got into the plane, the pilot asked if one of us would like to come and sit up front. Joan was up like a shot and as we got going she said to the pilot, 'Right, you can tell him now.'

Well, I was amazed and thrilled. We were to have a millionaire weekend at a luxury country hotel near Cheltenham in Gloucestershire. It was a beautiful five star hotel, formerly a countryseat in a parkland setting, that was frequented by top politicians, millionaires and film stars, and we had three luxury cars at our disposal (with full tanks, of course). The pilot saw to everything. He apologized for the absence of his employer, whose guests we were, and said he had been charged with taking care of us on his behalf, and after being booked in, we had a five-course dinner hosted by our pilot. But I was still bewildered and it wasn't until we went to our suite that Joan said, 'Right, now I'll tell you. This weekend is a prize which had been run by the Sheffield Property Guide and won by someone in Sheaf Market.' Joan had bought it off the winner, who was unable to use it as she had already arranged a holiday for the same weekend. Our host was the personal pilot and chauffeur to the owner of the property guide (and would fly him to his estate in Jersey or to Spain because he loved the shellfish there) and he was always on call. And when he flew us back on the Sunday evening, he took a diversion over Neepsend Ski Village and the Peak District. It was a truly fabulous weekend.

Looking back, I think how ironic life can be. Joan and I had created a beautiful home together and she had died too early to fully enjoy it. We both loved that house and it just wasn't the same there without her. Two years later I sold it, too many memories to live with. Now I wish I hadn't. But we all know about hindsight.

It is April 2011 and I am now 77 years old. The house I live in today belongs to my brother Lawrence, and I live alone, apart from my dog Sam. (My daughter Marilyn bought him for me. He is a long-haired dachshund and he thinks the world of me.) I still get out and about and try to be involved in some enterprise or other, and I'm mindful of a friend named Fred Russell, one of the nicest men I've ever met (his wife was a dragon). Fred had had a small manufacturing business in Brown Lane, just off Eyre Street, and had been one of my sources of work. He lived in a beautiful bungalow at Stannington. Occasionally I would go up there and we'd sit talking for hours, mainly politics and putting the world to rights. He said he thought I should have got involved with local politics but I told him I'd been too busy trying to earn a living. One night I asked him how he came into the cutlery business after working until his retirement as an engineer/manager at Mushet Tools Ltd on Penistone Road. He told me, 'Making cutlery, especially cheap cutlery, is just another form of engineering and there's no special skill or mystique involved.' And then he gave me a piece of advice that I haven't forgotten: 'If you're looking for something to get involved in, let it be something you've never done before, that way you'll enjoy it'. Very good advice and I'm following it.

Me and Joan with our very good friend Gerry

Flo, Gerry and Joan at Denby Dale festival

AFTERWORD

So at last I have finished; I think that this time I really have written the last page of the story of my life. I've tried to remember every aspect and include it here – the good, the bad and the ugly, some of which I'm proud and much of which I'm a little ashamed. I am ashamed of the way I behaved towards my first wife, Mary, when I met Joan and that I denied that there was someone else in my life. It was the coward's way.

I always used to say to myself as a kid that I would never make my own children do the things I had to do as a young boy: knocking on doors selling, and hawking and shouting round the streets with a pony and cart, instead of being at school. But, on the whole, it wasn't all bad and it taught me to stand on my own two feet. When I've tried to tell my son what my life was like, he would say that he wouldn't have done it. My reply was that I was helping to put bread on the table. However, my son and daughters are wonderful parents to their own children.

But I do believe that there's some truth in what my mother always said: "The 'arder tha is the more they'll think on tha." My brothers and sisters and I thought the world of my mother and father and were, all of us, always there for them.

When I ask myself what kind of person I have turned out to be, I'm not sure. I don't think it's for me to say, it's for others to decide. And I always think of what someone else much wiser than me said a long time ago: "Give me the boy till the age of seven and I will give you the man." I was my dad's right-hand man, even as a boy.

It's been a lonely life since I lost Joan; I miss her so much. But it's negative to sit around feeling sorry for yourself. Since last Christmas I've been lost as to what to do next, but a couple of months ago I had a very good idea: I've purchased a small fairground organ and I go busking with it, playing Sheffield city centre collecting for charities – St. Luke's Hospice, Bluebell Children's Hospice and others. And I am really enjoying doing so.

Well, I've already remembered more that I could have included in this book but my editor Laura (a lovely person) warned me off from the start – 'No more anecdotes, Derek, please.' And besides, I wanted to see it finished and in print. I hope you have found it a good read.

Myself and my wife Joan.
Madiera early 1990's.